# ESSENTIAL

## Family Law

ESSENTIAL

**Titles in the series:**

Company Law
Constitutional & Administrative Law
Contract Law
Criminal Law
EC Law
English Legal System
Family Law
Jurisprudence
Land Law
Tort
Trusts

# ESSENTIAL

## *Family Law*

by

Keith Morgan, LLB
Lecturer in Law
Swansea Law School

First published in Great Britain 1995 by Cavendish Publishing Limited, The Glass House, Wharton Street, London WC1X 9PX

Telephone: 0171-278 8000      Facsimile: 0171-278 8080

British Library Cataloguing in Publication Data

Morgan, K
Essential Family Law –
(Essential Law Series)
I Title II Series
344.20615

ISBN 1-85941-128 2
Printed and bound in Great Britain

**TO PAULINE, JOANNE, LYNNE AND DANIEL**

# Foreword

This book is part of the Cavendish Essential series. The books in the series are designed to provide useful revision aids for the hard-pressed student. They are not, of course, intended to be substitutes for more detailed treatises. Other textbooks in the Cavendish portfolio must supply these gaps.

Each book in the series follows a uniform format of a checklist of the areas covered in each chapter, expanded treatment of 'Essential' issues looking at examination topics in depth, followed by 'Revision Notes' for self-assessment.

The team of authors bring a wealth of lecturing and examining experience to the task in hand. Many of us can even recall what it was like to face law examinations!

Professor Nicholas Bourne
General Editor, Essential Series
Swansea Law School

Summer 1994

# Acknowledgments

I would like to express my thanks to my wife Pauline for her help and encouragement during the preparation of this book and the advice and experience provided by my daughter Lynne. I should also wish to express by thanks to Maureen, the Swansea Law School secretary, whose help was an essential element in the preparation of this book.

# Preface

The aim of this book is to assist students in their preparation for family law examinations. It will deal with the six major areas that are frequently examined and students are provided with a checklist and comprehensive notes on each of these essential issues.

The book contains up-to-date information and analysis of relevant cases and legislation which will be necessary for success.

The book should be read in conjunction with the Cavendish Lecture Notes Series, the leading text books recommended for particular courses, the law reports and other authoritative sources of information and opinion.

Students should remember that the knowledge gained should be put to the best use by proper analysis of examination questions and the relevant application of their knowledge to matters raised by the examiners.

Keith Morgan

# 1 Nullity

**You should be familiar with the following areas:** ✓

- void marriages (s 11 Matrimonial Causes Act 1973)
- voidable marriages (s 12 Matrimonial Causes Act 1973)
- bars where marriage is voidable (s 13 Matrimonial Causes Act 1973)

Although less than 1% of marriages are now terminated by nullity petitions today examiners still require a knowledge of this area.

Nullity falls into two categories – void and voidable marriages. Each area has its own concepts and grounds for its existence.

## Void marriages

There are social and public policy reasons as to why the marriage should not exist, as illustrated by the grounds contained in s 11 Matrimonial Causes Act (MCA) 1973.

Marriages celebrated after 31 July 1971 shall be void on the following grounds.

### Section 11(a)(i)
That the parties to the marriage are within the prohibited degrees of relationship; either blood relations (consanguinity) or non-blood relations (affinity).

Under the former the immediate family ie parents, grandparents, aunts and uncles, and siblings are prohibited from inter-marrying. Under the latter step-parents and parents-in-law are prohibited except under limited circumstances as are adoptive parents.

**Section 11(a)(ii)**

That either party is under the age of 16. However, if both parties are domiciled abroad at the time of the marriage it will be recognised as valid if the marriage is recognised as valid in the country in which it was celebrated.

In *Alhaji Mohammed v Knott* (1968) a Nigerian man married a 13-year-old girl. Both were domiciled in Nigeria. The marriage was valid in Nigeria, therefore it was valid in the UK when they later became domiciled here.

If either party is aged over 16 but under 18 then consent is required from certain people:

- each parent or guardian with parental responsibility for the child. This does not include an unmarried father who has not acquired parental responsibility;
- each person with a residence order in force for the child;
- if a court order exists then the consent of the local authority.

However, if this consent is lacking then the marriage will not be void unless the parents have publicly objected to the banns thereby voiding the banns. An application can also be made to the High Court, county court, or magistrates' court to obtain consent if consent cannot be obtained because of the parents absence or inaccessibility.

**Section 11(a)(iii)**

That the parties have intermarried in disregard to certain requirements as to the formation of marriage.

Publicity has been deemed necessary to prevent clandestine marriages as is illustrated by the existing rules which are complex and dealt with here only in outline.

## Church of England weddings

Banns have to be read three times in the required churches and then the parties may marry in one of the churches where the banns were read. Anyone publicly objecting to these banns causes the banns to be void.

Marriage can also take place after the granting of a common licence which requires that one of the parties has resided in the parish district for 15 days immediately prior to the granting of the licence. An affidavit is also required stating that there is no lawful impediment to the marriage and that the requirements of residence and consent are met.

The Archbishop of Canterbury may also grant a special licence which allows the marriage to take place any where at any time.

A marriage may also take place after the granting of a Superintendent Registrars' Certificate. This requires seven days residence and a solemn declaration that no lawful impediment exists and residence and consent requirements have been met. An entry is put in the marriage notice book and is open to public inspection for 21 days, then a certificate may be issued. This procedure is also used for non-Anglican marriages as is the issue of a Superintendent Registrars' certificate with a licence. This requires 15 days' residence in the district, and the notice entered in the marriage notice book. The marriage can take place one clear day after this notice has been given.

A Registrar General's Licence allows marriage at any named place because of the serious illness of one of the parties but, since the Marriage Act 1983 which allows marriage of the housebound and those detained in their home or place of confinement on the issue of a Superintendent Registrars' Certificate, is rarely used.

Anglican marriages must take place in the church where the banns were published or where authorised by the various licences and must be conducted by a clergyman in the presence of two witnesses.

## Other marriages

Non-Anglican marriages must take place in a building registered by the Registrar General as a 'place of meeting for religious worship' and be conducted by a minister of the religion concerned in the presence of two witnesses.

Civil marriages take place in a registry office in the presence of the Superintendent Registrar and are registered in the presence of witnesses.

When there are defects in the formalities the marriage will only be void if they are done 'knowingly and wilfully' by both parties.

This is the case if no certificate or licence has been issued, or where the marriage takes place in a church other than where the banns were published or over three months after the banns were published.

Where the banns have not been properly published the marriage may be void. This can happen if someone has publicly objected to the banns or there has been a false description of one of the parties. In the latter circumstances the cases of *Dancer v Dancer* (1948) and *Small v Small* (1923) can be compared and the intention behind the false description can be judged and a decision will be made if the banns are properly published. In the former there was held to be no attempt to deceive or hide the party's identity whereas in the latter there was such an attempt.

The situation in relation to false information being given to obtain a Superintendent Registrars' Certificate and licence is different as the aim is not to obtain publicity but to keep a public record and so the marriage will not generally be void (*Puttick v AG* (1979)).

It must be remembered that a defect does not necessarily void a marriage.

Consent is such an area and the necessity of showing that both parties know of the defect and wilfully partake in the ceremony also illustrates the point.

### Section 11(b)

That at the time of the marriage either party was already lawfully married.

This section requires the parties to fulfil the definition of marriage contained in *Hyde v Hyde* (1866) ie 'The voluntary union for life of one man and one woman to the exclusion of all others'.

The case of *Maples v Maples* (1987) illustrates that if a party has entered a valid marriage then to terminate that marriage and be able to enter another the termination must also be valid.

### Section 11(c)

That the parties are not respectively male and female.

The cases arising in this area normally concern a party who has undergone surgery for a sex change.

In *Corbett v Corbett* (1970) Laura Ashley, born a man, had undergone such an operation and then went through a ceremony of marriage with another man. It was held that a person's biological sex is fixed at birth and cannot be changed by artificial means.

This decision was followed by *Rees v UK* (1990) a case before the European Court of Human Rights which stated that the ruling had not violated European Convention on Human Rights. This was also the decision in *Cossey v UK* (1991).

### Section 11(d)

That in the case of a polygamous marriage entered into outside England and Wales that either party was at the time of the marriage domiciled in England or Wales.

In this situation a marriage is polygamous if it is actually polygamous or potentially polygamous.

Section 47 MCA allows matrimonial relief or a declaration concerning validity of a marriage entered into under a law allowing polygamy (matrimonial relief included nullity, divorce, judicial separation and matters relating to maintenance provisions). This supersedes the position under *Hyde* which was that English courts refused relief in polygamous marriages. However, there have been cases where s 11(d) has not applied.

In *Radwan v Radwan (No 2)* (1972) the husband was domiciled in Egypt and married his first wife, an Egyptian domiciled woman, in Cairo. He later married his second wife, an English domiciled woman in Paris intending to enter into a polygamous marriage according to Egyptian law and intending to live in Egypt. They did live in Egypt but later moved to, and became domiciled in, England. The second wife later petitioned for divorce.

The court held that as the second marriage was valid in Egypt and they had intended to live there it was valid in England. The court said s 11(d) did not apply.

In *Hussain v Hussain* (1982) even though there was a potentially polygamous marriage, both parties had no capacity to marry again and s 11(d) did not apply so the marriage was valid.

## Voidable marriages

Voidable marriages are defective but it is for the parties involved to decide whether or not they will end the marriage. The marriage will continue until it is avoided by way of a decree.

Section 16 MCA 1973 says that a decree of nullity granted after 31 July 1971 on the ground that a marriage is voidable, will only annul the marriage with respect to any time after the decree has been made absolute and the marriage will be treated as it if had existed up to that time notwithstanding the decree.

In *Ward v Secretary of State for Social Services* (1990) the husband, a naval officer, died in 1982 and the wife, as his widow, was entitled to a pension. This would cease if she re-married. This she did in 1986 but the marriage only lasted a week and was not consummated and so W was able to obtain a decree of nullity under s 12(a) MCA 1973. When her pension was stopped she argued that as her marriage had been avoided she was still entitled to the pension. Section 16 MCA clearly covers this situation and her marriage had been valid prior to the decree.

This was also the situation in the recent case of *P v P* (1994) where it was held that the marriage did subsist after a decree nisi had been granted and was only annulled after the decree had been made absolute. This case involved an appeal against an ouster order made against the wife. Part of the case revolved around the fact that a decree nisi had been granted and this led the judge to consider the marriage to be over. He then failed to deal with the wife's application under the Matrimonial Homes Act 1983 as he should have ie by consideration of the factors in s 1(3) of that Act. The Court of Appeal held that s 16 MCA 1973 provided that a marriage was annulled only with respect to any time after the decree absolute had been granted and that the wife's application should have been dealt with on that basis.

The grounds for marriages formed after 31 July 1971 being voidable are contained in s 12 MCA 1973.

### Section 12(a)
That the marriage has not been consummated owing to the incapacity of either party to consummate it.

### Section 12(b)
That the marriage has not been consummated owing to the wilful refusal of the respondent to consummate it.

The difference in the wording of these grounds shows that under s 12(a) a party can petition on his or her own incapacity but under s 12(b) cannot petition on his or her own wilful refusal.

Consummation occurs as soon as parties have sexual intercourse after the marriage. Sexual intercourse before marriage does not amount to consummation. The degree of sexual intercourse required was defined in *D v A* (1845):

Sexual intercourse in the proper meaning of the term is ordinary and complete intercourse; it does not mean partial and imperfect intercourse.

Incapacity in s 12(a) arises not only if the cause is incurable but also if the cure is by way of an operation which is dangerous or has little chance of success and the respondent refuses to undergo treatment. Before gaining the petition the petitioner must also show that the incapacity existed at the time of the marriage and at the time of the hearing there is no possibility of the marriage being consummated.

In *Napier v Napier* (1915) the wife had an operation six days before the hearing. The court adjourned to await the result of the operation.

However, psychological inability can also be seen as incapacity. For this to occur, it must amount to an 'invincible repugnance to sexual intercourse' because of an psychiatric or sexual aversion.

In *Singh v Singh* (1971) the wife met the husband for the first time at the arranged marriage. She refused sexual intercourse because she didn't like the look of him! The petition was refused, there was no incapacity involved. There was no aversion amounting to repugnance.

## Wilful refusal

This is defined in *Horton v Horton* (1974) as 'a settled and definite decision come to without just excuse'.

This can arise in a number of ways such as a psychological problem which does not amount to incapacity and the refusal to undergo an operation to remedy a physical defect preventing consummation but this must meet the definition ie be a settled and definite decision without just cause.

This may need an examination of the history of the marriage as in *Ford v Ford* (1987). Here, the husband was serving five years imprisonment. He refused to consummate the marriage that had taken place in prison even though he had had opportunities by being left alone with his wife. When the husband left prison he made it clear that he had no intention of returning to his wife and went to live with his girlfriend.

The petition was granted. His refusal in prison was not sufficient for wilful refusal. Consummation would have been against prison rules but his obvious intention not to take part in married life with his wife was sufficient.

Wilful refusal can also occur by a party refusing to carry out an essential arrangement eg a religious ceremony following a civil ceremony as required in some religions, knowing that the other party will refuse sexual intercourse until its done.

In *Jodla v Jodla* (1960) and *Kaur v Singh* (1972) the husbands refused to complete religious ceremonies in both cases knowing that by doing so their partners would refuse to consummate the marriage. It was held to be wilful refusal to consummate by the husband. However, full consideration of the situation is necessary as in *A v J (Nullity)* (1989). In this case the marriage was arranged between two Indian families. There was a civil ceremony to be followed four months later by a religious ceremony. The husband went abroad on business soon after the civil ceremony but returned for the religious ceremony. The wife refused his apology for his bad behaviour in going abroad and refused to go through with religious ceremony. The husband petitioned on wilful refusal. The Court held that the husband had behaved badly but had been sincere in his apology. The wife had been uncompromising in her attitude and refusal to go on with the religious ceremony which was seen as essential for cohabitation. The petition was granted.

### Section 12(c)

Lack of consent: that either party did not validly consent whether in consequence of duress, mistake, unsoundness of mind or otherwise.

Mistake can invalidate a marriage but will only do so if it concerns the nature of the ceremony or the identity of the other party. Mistakes as to the attributes of the other party will not invalidate it.

In *Mehta v Mehta* (1945) the petitioner thought the ceremony was a conversion to Hinduism. The marriage was void. In *Way v Way* (1949) the petitioner incorrectly thought that the marriage would allow the wife to leave Russia. The marriage was valid. The mistake was only about the effect of the ceremony, not its nature.

Although it seems unlikely that there could be a mistake as to another's identity, in the Australian case *C v D* (1979) it was said to have occurred. The petitioner's marriage to a hermaphrodite was annulled. She thought she had married a male; it was held to be a mistake of identity.

In *C v C* (1942) the husband represented himself as a well-known boxer. The wife petitioned on lack of consent because of her mistake. The petition was refused, her mistake was only that of the man's attributes, not his identity.

In *Militante v Ogunwomoju* (1993) the petitioner married a man in 1991 who went by the name of Ogunwomoju. This was an assumed name and he was an illegal immigrant. He was later deported and the petitioner sought a decree of nullity based on the fact that she had been mistaken as to his identity.

It was held that fraud going to the identity of the person vitiates consent and renders the marriage voidable. Decree granted.

## Unsoundness of mind

The basic test is does the party understand the nature of the ceremony? The concept of marriage is a simple one (*Durham* (1885)) and does not need a high level of understanding. All that is needed is that each party recognises the duties and responsibilities of marriage (*In the Estate of Park* (1953)).

There is a rebuttable presumption that once the marriage ceremony has been performed there has been valid consent by both parties and it is rare for this ground to succeed.

## Duress

Duress is said to be fear which is so overbearing that the element of free consent is absent.

In *Szechter v Szechter* (1971) it was said that it must amount to:

... a genuine and reasonably held fear caused by the threat of immediate danger (for which the party himself if not responsible) to life, limb or liberty, so that the constraint destroys the reality of consent.

However, in *Hirani v Hirani* (1982) it was said that this was not to be taken literally. All that it was necessary to show was that the threats or pressure are such that true consent is absent.

Here it is useful to compare *Singh v Singh* (1971) and *Hirani v Hirani* (1982).

In *Singh* the daughter entered into arranged marriage because of respect for her parents and tradition. No duress.

In *Hirani* the daughter entered into an arranged marriage under the threat of being forced to leave home. She was 19 years old and totally dependent on her parents. Duress.

It is generally accepted that a subjective test is to be applied in this situation ie has the petitioner been affected by the pressure, not would an ordinary person of firm standing be affected (*Scott v Sebright* (1866)).

### Section 12(d)
This section deals with a party suffering from a mental disorder. In this situation a party can give a valid consent and because of this the marriage cannot be avoided by s 12(c) but the party is not fit for marriage because of the mental disorder.

The mental disorder, which can be continuous or intermittent, must be within the Mental Health Act 1983.

### Section 12(e)
That at the time of marriage the respondent was suffering from VD in a communicable form.

### Section 12(f)

That at the time of the marriage the respondent was pregnant by some person other than the petitioner.

If the situation arises where the respondent wishes to prevent a decree of nullity being granted then the use of s 13 MCA 1973 must be considered.

## Bars when marriages are voidable

These are contained in s 13 MCA 1973.

### Section 13(1)

The court shall not grant a decree of nullity on the ground that a marriage is voidable if the respondent satisfies the court:

- That petitioner with knowledge that it was open to him to have the marriage avoided, so conducted himself in relation to the respondent as to lead the respondent reasonably to believe that he would not seek to do so.
- That it would be unjust to the respondent to grant the decree.

This means the respondent has to satisfy three requirements: knowledge; behaviour; unjust to grant the decree.

   (a) The petitioner knew he had the ability to avoid marriage.
   (b) The petitioner behaved in a way leading the respondent to reasonably believe he would not avoid marriage.
   (c) It would be unjust to the respondent to grant the decree.

   (a), (b) and (c) are conjunctive as shown in *D v D* (1979) where it was said that the husband's conduct and knowledge were seen as sufficient to have been a bar but the fact that there was no injustice to the wife prevented the bar operating and a decree was granted.

### Section 13(2)

The MCA provides time limits for grounds of s 12 (c)(d)(e) or (f) and no decree shall be granted unless:

- proceedings are instituted within three years of the date of the marriage; or
- leave has been granted under s 13(4).

### Section 13(3)

This requires that no decree be granted under s 12 (e) or (f) unless P can show that he was ignorant at the time of the marriage of the alleged fact.

**Section 13(4)**

This allows leave to be granted for proceedings to be instituted out of time if the court:

- is satisfied the petitioner has at some time during that period suffered from a mental disorder within MHA 1983; and
- considers that in all the circumstances of the case it would be just to grant leave for the institution of proceedings.

# Revision Notes

Marriages celebrated after 31 July 1971 are *void* on the following grounds.

## Section 11

Matrimonial Causes Act 1973. Void marriages.

## Section 11(a)

It is not a valid marriage under the provisions of the Marriage Acts 1949 and 1970.
(i)   Prohibited degrees of relationship. Consanguinity – ties by blood. Affinity – ties other than by blood.
(ii)  Either party is under the age of 16 (*Alhaji Mohammed v Knott* (1968)).
(iii) The parties have intermarried in disregard to certain requirements as to the formation of marriage.

Not all such matters will necessarily void the marriage:
* parental consent;
* false information to gain a superintendent;
* registrar's certificate;
* *Puttick v AG* (1979).

## Section 11(b)

At the time of marriage either party was already lawfully married.
* Definition of marriage (*Hyde v Hyde* (1866)).
* A valid marriage must be validly ended.
* *Maples v Maples* (1987).

## Section 11(c)

The parties are not respectively male and female.

## Section 11(d)

In the case of a polygamous marriage entered into outside England and Wales, that either party was at the time of the marriage domiciled in England or Wales.

- *Radwan v Radwan (No 2) (1972)*.
- *Hussain v Hussain (1982)*.

Marriages celebrated after 31 July 1971 are *voidable* on the following grounds.

## Section 12

Matrimonial Causes Act 1973. Voidable marriages.

## Section 12(a)

The marriage has not been consummated owing to the incapacity of either party to consummate it.

### Definition of sexual intercourse

- *D v A* (1845).

### Incapacity can be physical
- *Napier v Napier* (1915).

### Incapacity can be psychological
- *Singh v Singh* (1971).

### The petition can petition on his own incapacity.

## Section 12(b)

The marriage has not been consummated owing to the wilful refusal of the respondent to consummate it.
- Direct wilful refusal (*Ford v Ford* (1987)).
- Indirect wilful (*Jodla v Jodla* (1960)).
- *A v J (Nullity)* (1989).

## Section 12(c)

That either party to the marriage did not validly consent to it, whether in consequence of duress, mistake, unsoundness of mind or otherwise.
- Mistake

*Mehta v Mehta* (1945).
*Way v Way* (1949).
*Militante v Ogunwomoju* (1993).

The mistake must be regarding the nature of the ceremony *not* the effect of the ceremony.

The mistake must be regarding the identity of the person *not* his attributes.

* Unsoundness of mind
  *Durham v Durham* (1885).
  *In the Estate of Park* (1953).
* Duress
  *Szchter v Szchter* (1971).
  *Singh v Singh* (1971).
  *Hirani v Hirani* (1982).

Apply a subjective test , not a literal meaning to the fear being entertained.

## Section 12(d)

That the time of the marriage either party, though capable of giving a valid consent, was suffering (whether continuously or intermittently) from mental disorder within the meaning of the Mental Health Act 1983 of such a kind or to such an extent as to be unfit for marriage.

## Section 12(e)

That at the time of marriage the respondent was suffering from venereal disease in a communicable form.

## Section 12(f)

That at the time of the marriage the respondent was pregnant by some person other than the petitioner.

## Section 13

Matrimonial Causes Act 1973.
Bars to a decree being granted.

## Section 13(1)

Requirements to be shown by the respondent:
* The petitioner had knowledge that he could avoid the marriage.
* The petitioner behaved in such a way that the respondent believed that he would not do so.

- It would be unjust to the respondent to grant the decree.
- These requirements are conjunctive.
- *D v D* (1979).

### Section 13(3) time limits

Three years.

### Section 13(4) leave

Can be granted out of time if:
- Petitioner has suffered from mental disorder within Mental Health Act 1983.
- Court considers it would be just.

# 2 Divorce

It must be remembered that in any question on divorce the date of marriage must be more than one year prior to the presentation of the petition or the absolute bar contained in s 3(1) MCA 1973 (as amended by s 1 Matrimonial and Family Proceedings Act 1984) will prevent the granting of the petition (*Butler v Butler* (1990)).

At present there is only one ground for divorce, that is 'that the marriage has broken down irretrievably' (s 1(1) MCA).

This must be shown to the court by satisfying one or more of the five facts contained in s 1(2) (*Buffery v Buffery* (1988)).

These are two separate requirements and both must be satisfied. If the petitioner proves one or more of the five facts the court must grant a decree unless it is satisfied that the marriage has not broken down irretrievably (s 1(4)). However, the court considers all the evidence of the case and can refuse a petition if it considers that either requirement has not been satisfied.

In *Buffery v Buffery* (1988) the marriage had been shown to have irretrievably broken down but the petitioner failed to satisfy the fact of behaviour. In *Biggs v Biggs* (1977) the fact of adultery had been proved but not the requirement of irretrievable breakdown.

# Adultery and intolerability

### Section 1(2)(a)

The elements of the definition of adultery must be known.

### Adultery

Voluntary sexual intercourse between a married person and a person of the opposite sex, who may or may not be married and who is not the other person's spouse.

A person cannot commit adultery if they are insane and a wife has not committed adultery if she has been raped. It must be voluntary (*Redpath v Redpath* (1950)).

The degree of sexual intercourse required for adultery is that some degree of penetration is achieved (*Dennis v Dennis* (1955)). (This can be compared with the degree of sexual intercourse required for consummation ie 'ordinary and complete').

Adultery is considered to be a serious matrimonial offence and as such a standard of proof higher than the normal civil standard of proof is required (*Bastable v Bastable* (1968)).

Obviously, inference and suspicion are not enough. Some types of evidence that have been considered are: the birth of a child, where there has been non-access by the husband, or a confession statement.

The 'intolerability' element of s 1(2)(a) must also be satisfied but there has been discussion as to whether or not there needs to be a connection between the adultery and the intolerability. The matter seems to have been settled by the Court of Appeal decision in *Cleary v Cleary* (1974). The words 'in consequence of the adultery' could not be read into the fact's requirements. In this case the petitioner forgave the wife's adultery but could not accept her behaviour (ie found it intolerable that she continued contact with the other man and went out at night leaving the children in the care of the husband). The test to be applied is subjective ie does this particular petitioner find it intolerable but there must be some evidence to support the petitioner's view.

Section 2(1), (2) MCA contains the reconciliation provision in a case of adultery and intolerability. If the parties live together for a period or periods exceeding six months after one party becomes aware of the other's adultery then the party petitioning will not be able to rely on the fact of adultery ie over six months cohabitation 'destroys' the fact.

# Behaviour

### Section 1(2)(b)

This fact is normally referred to as 'unreasonable behaviour'. However, the aspect of `unreasonableness' must be considered in relation to whether or not the petitioner is expected to live with the respondent and not to the standard of behaviour.

This can be shown by the case of *Ash v Ash* (1972) where Bagnall J said 'it seems to me that a violent respondent, a petitioner who is addicted to drink, can reasonably be expected to live with a respondent similarly addicted'.

The correct test to be applied in 'behaviour' cases has been clearly stated in *Livingstone-Stallard v Livingstone-Stallard* (1974) where Dunn J suggested the 'jury approach' ie the direction a judge would give a jury:

... would any right thinking person come to the conclusion that this husband has behaved in such a way that this wife cannot reasonably be expected to live with him, taking into account the whole of the circumstances and the characteristics and personalities of the parties?

This can be summarised as a two part test combining an objective test of the behaviour and a subjective test of the parties personalities.

In the case of *Birch v Birch* (1992) it was first decided that although the marriage had been shown to have irretrievably broken down the court was of the opinion that the fact of behaviour, considered on an objective test, had not been satisfied.

The unsupported evidence of the wife was that the husband drank to excess and was boorish towards her, insulted her and made bigoted remarks concerning the fact she had been born in Ireland. The husband rejected the allegations.

On appeal, it was stated that the incorrect approach had been taken. The correct test was that in *Livingstone-Stallard v Livingstone-Stallard*. Take an objective view of the behaviour and consider it in the light of a subjective test of the parties nature. Here, the husband was bombastic, overbearing and chauvinistic and the wife was quiet and sensitive. She could not reasonably be expected to live with the respondent and the decree was granted.

The 'behaviour' fact has been, along with adultery, the most popular with petitioners for many years and has been used in approximately 36% of cases during the last 25 years. This has led to a considerable amount of case-law and questions on this fact are popular with examiners as they require the student to be able to apply the correct test to the circumstances and give a balanced argument on a wide range of behaviour which has been considered by the courts.

Some examples of the types of behaviour that have been considered include:

## Violence

In *Ash v Ash* (1972) the husband accepted that he had been violent and was an alcoholic. In *Bergin v Bergin* (1983) the wife had accepted violence for a number of years without reporting it. She now considered she had suffered enough and petitioned for divorce. It was clear that the fact of behaviour had been satisfied.

## Illness

This area of behaviour brings about the need to consider if the behaviour needs to be voluntary or can involuntary behaviour suffice? Also to be considered is the balance to be sought between the burden the petitioner can be expected to bear as part of his marital duty and how much of this burden he is able to bear.

In *Katz v Katz* (1972) a husband was a manic depressive and as a result of his abnormal behaviour his wife was driven to attempt suicide. The decree was granted after considering the responsibilities of marriage and the wife's ability to cope with the husband's behaviour, after making allowances for the husband's disability.

In *Thurlow v Thurlow* (1975) it was considered whether behaviour of a positive or negative nature was sufficient for a decree along with the fact that in some circumstances the behaviour, being caused by illness or injury may be involuntary.

The factors to be considered were the petitioner's marital duty to bear the burden of her spouse's illness, her ability to cope with the situation, the length of time it was likely to last and the effect it could have on her health.

It was also stated in this case that if the respondent had been reduced to a vegetative state, probably permanent in nature, then the petitioner would face considerable difficulty in satisfying the fact of behaviour. This shows that negative behaviour eg refusing to talk to the petitioner for long periods can satisfy the ground but the total lack of 'behaviour' would not.

## Cumulative effect of minor incidents

The behaviour involved in these circumstances would involve incidents in themselves trivial or seemingly unimportant, but the cumulative effect of which would have a serious, adverse effect on the petitioner. This was shown in *Livingstone-Stallard v Livingstone-Stallard* (1974) where the husband repeatedly belittled his wife in public, and was boorish and overly critical.

In *O'Neill v O'Neill* (1975) the husband questioned the children's paternity and spent a number of years carrying out 'home improvements' to the family home such as removing toilet doors and floorboards. The decree was granted on appeal as, after making allowances for the normal ups and downs of married life, there was a limit on what a spouse is expected to suffer.

When considering these examples of behaviour you should quote them to the best advantage to support your conclusions. Do not recite all the examples you can remember, use those that are relevant or illustrative.

## Reconciliation provisions

Section 2(3) contains the reconciliation provisions for this fact. If the parties have lived together for period(s) amounting to less than six months since the date of the last incident relied upon to petition then this will be disregarded when considering whether the petitioner can reasonably be expected to live with the respondent. However, if they cohabit for more than six months then this will be considered by the court when deciding whether or not it is reasonable to expect the petitioner to live with the respondent.

Here it would be useful to compare *Bradley v Bradley* (1973 and *Savage v Savage* (1982).

In the former case the parties had continued living together through force of circumstances. The wife could not get rehoused until after the divorce and was unable to get her violent husband to leave their present home. Decree granted.

In the latter case the parties resumed cohabitation three months after the wife had been granted a decree nisi. The cohabitation lasted for 3 ½ years. The court, on examining the circumstances of the case and the cohabitation refused to grant the decree absolute.

# Desertion

### Section 1(2)(c)

There are said to be four requirements to prove the fact of desertion. They are:

- the fact of separation;
- that the respondent intends to permanently desert the petitioner;
- the petitioner does not consent to the respondent leaving;
- the party who has left has done so without just cause.

The last of these requirements is not specifically mentioned in the Act but it is accepted as necessary as it is doubted that a court would find desertion to exist if the spouse did have just cause to leave.

### Separation

What is necessary is for someone to withdraw from the state of married life as in the case of *Price* (1970).

Here, whilst the husband was in hospital the wife decided to leave him and started divorce proceedings. The husband then decided to leave the wife and whilst she was on holiday he took his belongings and left the home. He was held to be in desertion whereas the wife had the intention but had not withdrawn.

The withdrawal is from a state of affairs not from a place.

In *Bradshaw v Bradshaw* (1897) the husband was a domestic servant in a large house. He was visited regularly by his wife and children but was held to be in desertion when he refused to see his wife on future visits. There need be no matrimonial home to leave.

However, if there is a matrimonial home then there must be a sufficient degree of separation shown to the court if the parties claim there to be two households under the same roof. There must be an end to the married state. This can be shown by a comparison of two cases: *Naylor v Naylor* (1961) and *Hopes v Hopes* (1948).

In the former case the wife performed no marital services for the husband and no element of communal or family life remained. There were separate households.

In the latter the wife performed no domestic duties for the husband but they did share meals and the house with the rest of the family. There was insufficient separation.

## The intention to permanently desert

The respondent's intention must be permanent when formed and the respondent will remain in desertion even if the desertion becomes involuntary.

In *Beeken v Beeken* (1948) the spouses became prisoners of war in 1942. The wife formed a relationship with another man in the camp and when she was about to be sent to another camp she informed her husband that she had no intention of returning to him. She was in desertion from that time.

## The petitioner must not consent

There are two elements concerned in this area:

- the petitioners must not agree to the respondent leaving; and
- the petitioner must not reject a reasonable offer of reconciliation by the respondent.

For the first element it is necessary for the petitioner to know that the respondent is leaving so communication of that fact is necessary.

In *Nutley v Nutley* (1970) the wife went to look after her elderly parents with her husband's consent. She later decided not to return to her husband but did not inform him of her decision. The husband later tried to divorce her using the original date on which the wife had left to see her parents. This was not allowed as he had consented to her leaving at that time.

It will not prevent desertion if the petitioner is glad to see the respondent leave but there is no consent (*Pizey v Pizey* (1961)).

## The petitioner must not give the respondent just cause to leave

This factor is not expressly mentioned in the Act but it is accepted that if there is just cause to leave there will be no desertion. The conduct will usually amount to 'grave and weighty' conduct as in *Lang v Lang* (1954) a case also occurring in constructive desertion.

Examples of this type of behaviour can be seen in cases such as *Marsden v Marsden* (1967) where the husband continually accused his wife of committing adultery without giving her an opportunity to answer in her defence. In *Timmins v Timmins* (1953) the husband was a boorish, bad-tempered man and assaulted his wife.

### Constructive desertion

This occurs when one party has left the home but has done so due to being driven out by the 'grave and weighty' conduct of the other party, who in reality, is the party responsible for the desertion (*Lang v Lang* (1954)). In this case the husband was held to have known that his conduct would mean his wife leaving and so he was held to be in constructive desertion.

There need be no intention to drive the other spouse out. The respondent may be unaware of the effect of his behaviour but will still be held to be in constructive desertion (*Gollins v Gollins* (1963)). It is important, however, to be able to show that the behaviour has influenced the spouse's decision to leave. If it did not effect the decision the spouse who has left may be found to be in desertion.

In *Herod v Herod* (1938) the wife left the husband prior to being aware of his adultery. She was held to be in desertion even though he had committed numerous acts of adultery.

### Reconciliation

When considering whether the 'continuous' element of the time requirement has been met s 2(5) MCA 1973 states that no account shall be taken of any period(s) of cohabitation not exceeding six months, but such period(s) will not count towards the period of desertion or the period of living apart. This means that if the spouses part then resume cohabitation for three months, then part again it must be shown that the period of two years, three months must have passed prior to the petition from the first occasion of them parting.

### Termination of desertion

Absolute defences:

- The granting of a decree of judicial separation or a valid separation agreement. These are seen as supervening consent.
- The refusal of a reasonable offer of reconciliation without just cause eg a party offering reconciliation but attaching unreasonable conditions eg in *Hutchinson v Hutchinson* (1963) there was to be no sexual intercourse.
- Resumption of cohabitation would amount to returning to a state of affairs where desertion would not have been found originally.

In *Batram v Batram* (1949) the wife was forced to return and share a house with the husband due to circumstances beyond her control but did not perform marital duties and treated him as a disliked lodger. Desertion continued.

In *Bull v Bull* (1953) the spouses resumed living together, the wife refused sexual intercourse but did other marital chores such as cooking and mending clothes. This was sufficient to end desertion on there being held to be one household existing under one roof.

## Discretionary defences

- Petitioner's implied consent to the separation by taking action to prevent the other spouse returning.
- The petitioner unsuccessfully petitioning for divorce or nullity, on other grounds.
- The petitioner's own adultery unless the respondent is indifferent to it.

# Separation

Section 1(2)(d) - two years separation and the respondent consents.
Section 1(2)(e) - five years separation.

The facts can effectively be dealt with together, the basic principles being the same apart from the length of time involved and the question of consent in s 1(2)(d).

## Separation

There must be more than mere physical separation. There also needs to be the mental element ie one or both of the parties must recognise the marriage as being at an end.

In *Santos v Santos* (1972) the husband lived in Spain, the wife in England. She visited him on a regular basis and it was unclear if they were living apart.

The recognition of the marriage being at an end can be made unilaterally, and need not be communicated to the other spouse. It is clear that this could cause hardship and the court will require evidence showing when such a decision was reached. This could be by way of oral evidence, a letter or the ending of regular visits. However, if the court only has the oral evidence of the petitioner it will treat such evidence with caution and look at the surrounding circumstances to see if there are any other indications as to when the period began.

## Separate households

Section 2(6) says that a husband and wife shall be treated as living apart unless they are living with each other in the same household. This means that we have to consider the question of separate households under the same roof.

The essential element is that it can be shown that there has been a change in the nature of the relationship. This can best be illustrated by comparing the cases of *Fuller v Fuller* (1973) and *Mouncer v Mouncer* (1972). In *Fuller* the wife left to live with another man. The husband later became ill and unable to care for himself. The wife agreed to take him into her new home as a lodger, paying for his keep and the domestic services, provided by the wife. It was clear that both had accepted that the marriage was at an end. They were held to be living apart in separate households.

In *Mouncer* the parties had separate bedrooms and did not get on well together but did share meals with the family. The husband wanted to leave but stayed because of the children. It was held that they were not living apart. The lack of a physical relationship and normal affection were insufficient evidence of separation. These factors apply to both s 1(2)(d) and s 1(2)(e), varying only in the length of time involved.

## Consent

The essential difference in these facts concerns the requirement of consent by the respondent in s 1(2)(d) only.

The petitioner has the burden of showing that the respondent has consented in the proper manner. This consent must be express and is normally given via a signed statement. The respondent should be given sufficient information to enable him to give a proper consent to the decree.

The court will not imply any element of consent. In *McGill v Robson* (1972) the husband said he wanted the proceedings to be dealt with as soon as possible but did not provide an express consent. The decree was refused as the court refused to imply consent.

As with all matters of consent there must be capacity (*Mason v Mason* (1972)). Again it is for the petitioner to show that the respondent has this capacity if there is any doubt.

The respondent can withdraw his consent at any time prior to the decree nisi (r 16(2) Matrimonial Causes Rules 1977). Also under s 10(1) MCA 1973 the respondent may apply to the court any time before decree absolute for the decree nisi to be rescinded if he can satisfy the court that he was misled by the petitioner, whether intentionally or not, on any matter which he took into consideration in giving his consent.

## Time requirements

These are strictly applied as shown by *Warr v Warr* (1975) and do not include the day of separation.

In s 1(2)(e) cases once the period of five years has been shown to exist then the respondent cannot be granted a decree (*Parsons v Parsons* (1975)).

## Reconciliation

### Section 2(5)

When considering the time period no account need be taken of any period(s) not exceeding six months during which the parties resumed living with each other.

# Provisions affecting the granting of decrees

### Section 5

If a decree absolute is granted on the basis of five years separation then s 5 MCA 1973 provides the respondent with a power to oppose the granting of a decree if it can be shown that the respondent would suffer grave financial or other hardship by the granting of the decree and that it would in all the circumstances be wrong to dissolve the marriage. Both elements must be satisfied.

The application is made prior to the decree nisi and the court will consider all the circumstances of the case including the conduct of the parties and their interests and those of any children or others.

This measure is intended to protect older wives who have brought up their families and would be in a precarious financial position if their husbands should obtain a divorce. In many cases this arises through the loss of pension provisions, which are usually only payable to wives, or widows, and the lack of job opportunities for the wife because of her age and lack of work experience.

## Grave financial hardship

It must be shown that the hardship must arise from the granting of the decree.

In *Talbot v Talbot* (1971) the spouses had separated in 1966. The wife obtained a decree of judicial separation and after five years the husband petitioned for divorce.

The wife used s 5 to oppose the petition but it was held that no hardship arose from the granting of the decree.

It was also stated in this case that the question of hardship was to be decided subjectively in relation to the particular marriage and then considered objectively.

The respondent also has to show the hardship is 'grave' which is to be given its ordinary meaning (*Reiterbund v Reiterbund* (1975)).

The usual example of 'grave financial hardship' arises through the loss of pension rights as was the case in *Parker v Parker* (1972). This case also illustrates how if a petitioner can compensate for that hardship then s 5 can be avoided and a decree obtained.

In *Parker* the respondent claimed that the loss of the possibility of a police widow's pension amounted to grave financial hardship. The court agreed. However, the petitioner was able to compensate for this loss by providing an annuity for the respondent. This provided another form of income for the respondent and although it did not compensate totally for the loss of the pension it did come very near to it.

In *Julian v Julian* (1972) the petitioner made an offer to try and compensate for the loss of pension rights but the court considered the offer to be inadequate as there was still a large gap between the offer being made and the pension entitlement if the husband should die.

These cases show that s 5 can be avoided but the compensation offered must be seen as adequate.

## Other hardship

This normally arises in cases where the respondent claims that she will be ostracised if the decree is granted as divorce is not acceptable in her section of society. It has yet to be successful but in *Banik v Banik* (1973) it was said that such claims do require investigation and should not be rejected out of hand.

In *Parghi v Parghi* (1973) the wife claimed such hardship but the court found that the parties were from a Hindu sect whose ideas were very close to those of western society and divorce was more accepted. The wife's claim failed.

## Wrong to dissolve the marriage

Even if the respondent can show 'grave financial or other hardship' it is also necessary to show that it would be wrong to dissolve the marriage. In *Brickell v Brickell* (1973) the respondent's wife was able to show grave financial hardship but because of her behaviour in spying on her husband and causing the failure of his business it was held that it would not be wrong to dissolve the marriage. The decree was granted.

This defence is available only in cases based on fact (s 1(2)(e)).

### Section 10

In cases based on the facts in s 1(2)(d) and (e) then the respondent can apply to the court for considerations of his or her financial provision on divorce. This provision is contained in s 10(2) MCA 1973. Section 10(3) empowers the court not to make the decree absolute unless it is satisfied that the petitioner need not make any financial provision or that the provision made is reasonable and fair or the best that can be made in the circumstances.

In reaching its decision the court will consider all the circumstances including the age, health, conduct of the parties, earning capacity and the financial resources and obligations of the parties.

In *Krystmann v Krystmann* (1973) the parties had married in Italy during the war but had separated after only two weeks before the husband returned to England. Twenty six years later he petitioned for divorce based on five years separation. Not surprisingly, the court decided that there was no need for any financial provision to be made in these circumstances as they had been apart for such a long period.

In *Lombardi v Lombardi* (1973) the court looked at the length of the marriage – five years, the length of separation – 10 years, and the parties respective financial positions and decided that his offer was reasonable and fair. The decree was made absolute.

In *Garcia v Garcia* (1992) it was stated that s 10(3) covered past as well as future financial provision. In this case the wife applied under s 10(2) for the decree absolute to be delayed until the husband had paid £4,000 outstanding to her son for maintenance and school fees. She did not want financial provision for herself.

The husband appealed, claiming that the payments being sought were for past provisions and s 10 concerned future needs. The appeal failed.

It was held that s 10 concerned past and future provisions, including correcting past obligations and remedying any failures to fulfil them.

However, under s 10(4) the court can make the decree absolute despite s 10(3) if the circumstances make it desirable to do so without delay or if it receives a satisfactory undertaking from the petitioner that he will make financial provisions for the respondent that the court may approve.

The undertaking must not be vague as the court must be able to enforce it. In the absence of specific proposals the court will decide on an appropriate order.

This provision only applies to divorces based on s 1(2)(d) and (e).

### Section 41

This provision applies to all divorces where there are children involved. It does not depend on the application of the respondent. Under this provision the court shall consider if there are any children of the family concerned and where there are such children, whether in the light of any proposed arrangements for the welfare of the children, it should exercise any of its powers under the Children Act 1989 with respect to any of them.

This provision is not often used as the parties are advised to make proper arrangements for the children prior to the presentation of the petition but can be used if there is conflict between the parties over the children's upbringing.

## Law Commission proposals for reform

### Family law: the ground for divorce – facing the future

#### Recommendations

Irretrievable breakdown is to be retained as the sole ground for divorce *but* should be proved by the expiry of a minimum period of 12 months for the consideration of the practical consequences resulting from divorce and reflection to see if the relationship is irreparable.

The period of consideration is started by a statement that one or both parties believe that the relationship has broken down. It is made on a prescribed form, under oath and the parties are then given an information pack.

During this period, counselling, conciliation and mediation are encouraged but the court will have the power to direct parties to attend an interview with a specified person or agency to give the parties an explanation of conciliation and a chance to participate. The Agency must then report back within a given time limit.

All statements during this procedure are privileged.

The court must make a preliminary assessment no later than 12 weeks after the original statement is made in order to monitor progress on any arrangements being made and make any orders, or exercise powers appropriate at that time.

The court will have six specific duties:

- identify any relevant children of the family and consider powers under the Child Act 1989;
- identify areas of dispute and how to resolve them;
- give directions for the conduct of any proceedings relating to issues not resolved;
- consider orders for financial provision of property adjustment already agreed by the parties;
- consider whether or not to extend the period on grounds of incapacity or delay in service;
- consider whether the hardship bar is likely to be raised and on what grounds.

During the period the court has powers to make orders re:

- children;
- financial provision/property adjustment on application or its own motion;
- violence and molestation;
- determine occupation of matrimonial home.

The period of consideration is *a minimum of 11 months*. It may be extended by the court, on application or on its own motion. Once it has elapsed there will be a transitional period of *one month making 12 months overall*. This would mean that no divorce would be granted within two years of the date of marriage as no period of consideration could begin within the first year of marriage.

# *Revision Notes*

## Divorce

### Matrimonial Causes Act 1973 (MCA 1973)

#### Section 1(1)
Irretrievable breakdown of marriage.
The *only* ground for divorce.

#### Section 1(2)
The five facts needed to illustrate irretrievable breakdown.
These are *separate* requirements, both must be satisfied.

#### Section 1(2)(a)

*Adultery and intolerability*

*Adultery*
- Sexual intercourse.
- Evidence.

*Intolerability*
- Independent requirement.
- Subjective test.

### Reconciliation provisions

#### Section 2(1)(2)
Six months cohabitation destroys the fact.

#### Section 1(2)(b) behaviour
Is it 'unreasonable' for the petitioner to live with the respondent?
Two part test, subjective and objective.
Behaviour must be found to be present, be it positive or negative, voluntary or involuntary.
Consider examples of behaviour considered in decided cases. Apply those which are relevant or comparable and bear in mind the burdens and responsibilities of marriage.

## Reconciliation provisions

### Section 2(3)
No absolute bar *but* time will be considered when judging 'unreasonable'.

### Section 1(2)(c)
- Desertion.
- Four requirements.

## Separation

- Permanent Intention to desert.
- Lack of consent.
- Separation without just cause.

## Separation

- Withdrawal from married life.
- State of affairs not a place.
- Separate households.

## Intention

It must be permanent. It continues even if later involuntary.

## No consent

The petitioner must not agree to the respondent leaving and the petitioner must not reject a reasonable offer of reconciliation made by the respondent.

The petitioner must be aware that desertion has occurred.

## Without just cause

This is not expressed in s 1(2)(c) but it is clear that desertion cannot exist if there is a just reason for a spouse to leave.

It overlaps with constructive desertion as if there is just cause, the other spouse could be judged to be in constructive desertion if their conduct is 'grave and weighty'.

There is no requirement for there to be any intention to drive out the other spouse.

### Section 1(2)(d)

Two years separation and the respondent's consent.

## Living apart

### Section 2(6)

... a husband and wife shall be treated as living apart unless ... living with each other in the same household.

There must be a mental element ie that at least one party has recognised that the marriage is at an end (*Santos v Santos* (1972)).

There must be physical separation but this can also exist where the parties reside under the same roof as long as there are two separate households. A change in the nature of the parties' relationship, ie they no longer live as husband and wife, must be shown (*Mouncer v Mouncer* (1972); *Fuller v Fuller* (1973)).

Consent is a vital element and a number of requirements need to be fulfilled.

Consent must be express in nature. The court will not imply any element of consent (*McGill v Robson* (1972)).

The respondent must have the capacity to consent.

It must not be obtained by the respondent being misled.

### Rule 16(2)

Matrimonial Causes Rules 1977 and s 10(1) MCA 1973 provide protection for the respondent.

The two year period is strictly construed (*Warr v Warr* (1975)).

## Reconciliation provisions

Period(s) not exceeding six months of resumed co-habitation will not be considered but do not count towards the two year period

The above factors also apply to s 1(2)(e) five years separation.

Once separation for five years has been admitted there are no grounds upon which the respondent can be granted a divorce.

## Provisions affecting the granting of decrees

### Section 10(2) and (3) MCA 1973

The respondent can ask the court, after the granting of a decree nisi, to consider his financial position and the court will not grant a decree absolute until it is satisfied:

- that the petitioner need make no financial provision for the respondent (*Krystmann v Krystmann* (1973));
- that the financial provision is reasonable (*Lombardi v Lomardi* (1973));
- is the best that can be made in the circumstances.

It applies to future *and* past circumstances (*Garcia v Garcia* (1992)).

However, the court may still grant a decree absolute because of the consideration in s 10(4) MCA 1973.

This provision is available for s 1(2)(d) and (e) only.

### Section 5(1) MCA 1973

These provisions were intended to protect the interests of older wives who needed financial security after long marriages.

The respondent can apply, prior to a decree nisi being granted, that the granting of a decree would cause grave financial or other hardship and it would in all the circumstances be wrong to dissolve the marriage.

Section 5(2) MCA 1973 contains the considerations to be made by the court.

The hardship must arise from the decree (*Talbot v Talbot* (1971)).

### Financial hardship

The provision includes the loss of pension rights but this defence can be overcome by alternative financial arrangements.
- *Parker v Parker* (1972).
- *Julian v Julian* (1972).

### Other hardships

Religious/social grounds that may arise on the granting of a decree due to the respondent's cultural/religious background.
- *Parghi v Parghi* (1973).

The second element, ie it would be wrong to dissolve the marriage, must be satisfied in addition to the hardship element.
- *Brickell v Brickell* (1973).

Cases illustrate the possible interplay between s 5 and s 10. If a s 5 defence fails consider a s 10 application to improve any financial provisions (*Balraj v Balraj*).

Section 5 defence is *only* available for s 1(2)(e).

**Section 41 MCA 1973**

This provision affects all divorces, decrees of nullity or judicial separation where children are involved.

The court must be satisfied in all cases affecting children that arrangements for the welfare of every child are satisfactory or are the best that can be devised or other factors exist.

## Reform

Law Commission proposals for reform. *The Ground for Reform – Facing the Future.*

- Irretrieveable breakdown retained as the sole ground.
- 11 month period – consideration of implications, counselling etc.
- One month period – transitional period.

The court will have certain duties and will set timetables and monitor progress.

# 3 Ancillary relief

The area of difficulty for students when dealing with ancillary relief is that of s 25, the considerations to assist the court. This statutory list aims to bring consistency to this area but it must be remembered that the importance of each factor will vary and in some questions some factors may be irrelevant. The application of the students knowledge in this area, if precise, can gain good marks. The type of order made will be decided following a valuation of the considerations.

## The welfare of minor children of the family (s 25(1))

The welfare of the children is not paramount under the MCA and will not override the other considerations. However, it is the first and most important consideration (*Suter v Suter and Jones* (1987)).

## Financial resources (s 25(2)(a))

The court will consider all the financial resources of the parties including those likely to arise in the future. In its consideration the court will look at the realistic situation and not just accept the parties evidence.

In *Hardy v Hardy* (1981) the husband was said to earn £70 per week. He was employed at his father's racing stables. The court considered he could earn a higher salary and made an order for £50 per week.

In *Newton v Newton* (1990) the court reached its decision on inferences drawn from the husband's life-style. He was said to have no income but financed himself by borrowing on property deals.

It is not only the husband's earning capacity that must be considered. In *Mitchell v Mitchell* (1984) the wife was an experienced secretary but now worked as a part-time canteen assistant. The court said it was reasonable to expect her to increase her earning capacity when the children left school, probably within three years and this affected the lump sum awarded to her.

## Earnings of a new partner

It must be remembered that the remarriage of the recipient of any order automatically ends periodical payments. Co-habitation is not equated with remarriage. If the potential payer of an order has a new partner then no order will be made if it can only be paid from the resources of the new partner. However, the existence of these resources will not be ignored by the court as they may well have the effect of releasing more of the payer's resources for paying any order made (*Macey v Macey* (1981). No order will be made if the potential payer has no income or means of his own.

In *Brown v Brown* (1981) the husband was unemployed and had no income whatsoever. He was entirely dependent on his mistress.

## Financial obligations (s 25(2)(b))

To ensure a fair balance the court will also look to the future when considering on-going obligations. The party who retains day-to-day responsibility for bringing up the children, usually the wife, has long-term obligations in many cases. An important factor is that of housing. As the welfare of the child is the first and most important factor this can often mean the partner bringing up the children being allowed to retain the house on a trust for sale until the youngest child reaches a stated age or leaves full-time education as in *Mesher v Mesher* (1980).

## Responsibilities of a new family

The court will avoid making crippling orders in these circumstances as the husband has a legal obligation to maintain his new family and the attitude has been to give these obligations adequate weight.

The court should consider the requirement of support for the first family and the man's ability to meet them but to do so in the light of the reality that the man has future hopes for a new family and reach a reasonable balance between the two demands.

In *Stockford v Stockford* (1982) the husband remarried and raised a second mortgage to buy a house for his new wife and child. The only capital he had was tied up in his first home which was occupied by his first family. The court decided that his first wife was now able to go out to work and the court reduced her maintenance to allow the husband to maintain his second family.

The court will see what is reasonable in all the circumstances in trying to achieve this balance between allowing the husband to acquire a second family whilst ensuring he fulfils his responsibilities to his first family.

## Standard of living (s 25(2)(c))

A fall in the standard of living of a family involved in a divorce is, in most cases, seen as inevitable. The court's approach is to distribute any such reduction evenly without bringing either party below subsistence level.

When dealing with wealthy families it is often possible for the court to settle matters without any significant drop in living standards. The court will consider the standard of living to which the parties have become accustomed and seek to maintain that standard.

In *Calderbank v Calderbank* (1975) the wife was very wealthy and she financed the family life including the children's education at private school. The husband was unemployed. He was awarded a lump sum to purchase a home suitable to his station in life and suitable for the children to visit.

Where a situation arises that a family has achieved an improved standard of living during the existence of the marriage the court has shown that it is willing to apply the higher standard.

In *Vicary v Vicary* (1992) the marriage lasted 15 years. At first the family lived frugally but the family business prospered and living standards rose significantly. The wife was given an order in keeping with the higher standard of living.

## Ages and duration of marriage (s 25(2)(d))

The ages of the parties can have an effect on the orders in as much as young couples are more likely to be involved in 'clean breaks' whilst older couples are more likely to make applications under ss 5 and 10 MCA 1973.

The duration of the marriage can also affect the type of order made. It must be remembered that even in very short marriages financial provisions can be made.

In *Brett v Brett* (1969) after a marriage of 5 ½ months a large order was made for the wife.

However, s 25A has always to be considered and if it is a short, childless marriage no order may be made or an order for a limited period only.

In *Attar v Attar (No 2)* (1985) the marriage lasted only six months and the wife received a lump sum equivalent to two years salary to allow her to re-adjust.

## Cohabitation prior to marriage

A factor to be considered in this area is that of cohabitation prior to marriage. The general attitude is that such cohabitation is irrelevant. This is especially so where there is a lack of commitment in the relationship.

In *H v H* (1981) the parties had an 'on and off' relationship for six years prior to their marriage which lasted seven weeks. The court ignored the period prior to the marriage but did make a lump sum to allow the wife to readjust. However, where commitment can be found between the parties the court will consider the period prior to marriage.

In *Kokosinski v Kokosinski* (1980) the parties had lived together for 22 years and had a son. They were unable to marry as the man was already married and could not obtain a divorce. Eventually he was free to marry but when they did so the marriage lasted for less than a year. The court was prepared to consider the whole period as the wife had shown commitment equivalent to that found in marriage and was awarded a large sum to enable her to purchase property.

## Physical or mental disability (s 25(2)(e))

Allowances will be made for such disability if it is possible to compensate by monetary means.

In *Jones v Jones* (1975) the wife was physically disabled following a knife attack by the husband and was unable to work. She was awarded the matrimonial home absolutely to provide her with some security for the future. However, if monetary means cannot compensate then no order may be made.

In *Seaton v Seaton* (1986) the husband suffered a severe heart attack and his quality of life was greatly impaired. He was looked after by his parents and received state benefits. Any order imposed on the wife for his benefit would be pointless, it would not improve his quality of life.

Some disabilities worsen as time passes and in these circumstances the court makes allowances.

In *Sakkas v Sakkas* (1987) the family's only asset was the home. When the husband developed multiple sclerosis he went to live with his sister, leaving the wife and children in the home. On divorce a Mesher order was made allowing the wife to occupy the home until the youngest child was 20 years old, it would then be sold but the shares would not be decided until that time as it would not be possible to assess the husband's needs until that time.

## Contributions to the family welfare (s 25(2)(f))

It must be remembered that both parties will contribute to the family welfare in differing ways, the husband by working and providing the money for everyday life whilst the wife cares for the children and looks after the family home. Each earns credit for their contributions which are positive but they can also be debited for any contributions that are considered to be negative.

This important consideration was brought to the fore by Denning LJ in *Wachtel v Wachtel* (1973). The importance given to this consideration is well illustrated by the case of *Smith v Smith* (1991).

The wife was awarded a £54,000 lump sum order as part of a clean break. She committed suicide six months later and the husband appealed against the order. The court considered that both parties had contributed equally during the marriage, both deserved recognition of their efforts. The wife had no future needs but the court decided to recognise her contribution by amending the order to £25,000 which would go to her estate.

The spouse's contribution to the family business will also be rewarded.

In *Gojkovic v Gojkovic* (1991) the wife's contribution to the family business was exceptional and in the court's opinion she was entitled to more than the £532,000 the husband had offered and awarded her £1 million.

These cases show how a positive contribution can be rewarded. The following case shows how a negative contribution can lead to a reduction in an order.

In *E v E* (1990) the wife neglected the children, had a number of adulterous affairs and abandoned the husband. The court saw this as a negative contribution and reduced the award she may have been given but kept in mind that she should not be put in financial difficulty as it would be against the children's interests. This case also illustrates the general attitude towards the next consideration.

## Conduct it would be inequitable to disregard (s 25(2)(g))

The courts attitude in this area is that of reluctance to examine the parties' conduct when trying to decide who is responsible for the breakdown as usually there is some element of fault on both sides. This is shown by *E v E* (1990) where the court took account of the wife's behaviour under s 25(2)(f) rather than s 25(2)(g). Conduct will be considered, however, where the court judges it to be 'both obvious and gross' and necessitates a reduction in an order.

Some examples of such behaviour seen as relevant by the court include abandoning a blameless spouse (*Robinson v Robinson* (1983)); violence (*Jones v Jones* (1975)); repugnant sexual behaviour (*Dixon v Dixon* (1974)).

If both parties are found to be equally guilty of such conduct then their conduct may be disregarded. In *Leadbeater v Leadbeater* (1985) the wife was an alcoholic and an adultress. The husband also committed adultery on a number of occasions and brought a 16-year-old girl into the household and committed adultery with her. The parties' conduct was considered to be equally bad and so irrelevant.

Normally, post-separation conduct is not considered as relevant and the couples are free to go their own way as the conduct would not have led to the breakdown. However, in extreme cases even post divorce conduct will be considered by the court and will affect any order granted.

In *Kyte v Kyte* (1987) the husband was a depressive and suicidal. The wife gained a divorce on the fact of his behaviour. The husband later found out that the wife had only obtained the divorce to enable her to live with another man with whom she had been having an affair.

The wife had previously failed to prevent her husband attempting suicide and on another occasion had actively encouraged him to do so. The court said that conduct had the contributed to the breakdown, either during or after the marriage and was relevant. Here the wife's conduct was both 'obvious and gross' and her lump sum order was reduced to £5,000 from £14,000.

## Loss of future benefit (s 25(2)(h))

This consideration usually involves the loss of occupational pensions and the cases that arise in relation to s 5 and s 10 provisions can be used in these circumstances (*Parker v Parker* (1972); *Julian v Julian* (1972)).

The importance of getting to know and understand the contents and application of s 25 cannot be over emphasised! Students must realise that it is the basis for the court's decision and that in practice this decision will affect the parties lives for many years to come. Thus it is an area that will almost certainly appear on every examination paper.

## Clean break provisions (s 25(A))

The idea behind these provisions is to bring to an end any dependence or obligation between the parties as soon as is practicable depending on the circumstances of the case.

The court has a duty to consider a 'clean break' in each case (*Barrett v Barrett* (1988)). It does not have to apply the provisions. It will look at the situation in three ways:

- Is a 'clean break' appropriate?
- If so, can it be granted immediately or after a period of adjustment?
- If not, should it be dismissed and an order made preventing further application for periodical payments?

### Section 25A(1)

The court sees a short childless marriage as the ideal situation for a 'clean break' (*Attar (No 2)* (1985)). However, it is not always ruled out if there are children of the family but it may be judged to be inappropriate; if there is any uncertainty as to the future then the children's interests will be considered and a nominal maintenance order will be made to allow future adjustments to be made to meet their needs. Uncertainty about a spouse's future may also make a 'clean break' inappropriate (*Suter v Suter and Jones* (1987)).

In *Scanlon v Scanlon* (1990) an older wife's health was causing concern and such an order was said to be inappropriate as she could be adversely affected by a deterioration in her health.

It may be easier to apply this provision if the family involved is wealthy and has sufficient assets to maintain the parties in the manner to which they have become accustomed and be given full credit for their past contributions (*Gojkovic v Gojkovic* (1990)

### Section 25A(2)

This applies where the court considers a 'clean break' to be the appropriate measure but only after a period of adjustment. If the spouse would have difficulty adjusting even after such a period then this order would not be made as in *M v M* (1987). The wife was 47 years old and had little or no work experience and would find it difficult to get well paid employment. The husband offered maintenance for five years. The court did not make an order under s 25A(2) as it considered that the wife would not be self-sufficient after five years and would suffer real hardship.

Another factor to be considered is that of any bitterness and acrimony between the parties. In *Evans v Evans* (1990) following a great deal of acrimony an order for maintenance was made for three years. By this time the children would be away at school and the wife would be able to exploit her full earning capacity and be self-sufficient. Such an order would avoid any future bitterness and difficulties.

### Section 25A(3)

This encourages a once and for all settlement and allows the court to make an order preventing a spouse from making future applications for periodical payments. In *Seaton v Seaton* (1986) the husband was severely disabled and lived with his parents. There was little point making an order against the wife as it would have no beneficial effect on his quality of life and an order was made preventing any further applications.

### Distribution of Assets

There have been a number of guidelines laid down to provide assistance to the courts.

### The one third principle

This arose in *Wachtel v Wachtel* (1973) where it was assumed that the husband would have greater expenses to bear than the wife eg bills, etc and so should receive two thirds of the family assets and the wife one third.

However, it must be remembered that this, along with all other guidelines, is not a rule and only gives a starting point that may require adjustment on full consideration of s 25. The one third principle is generally of use in middle-income cases.

## The 'net effect' approach

The case of *Stockford v Stockford* (1982) suggested this approach. It was not to look at any given situation in just a mathematical way but to look at the reality. Look at the difference between the top line and bottom line of any pay slip! This illustrates the reality.

## The Duxbury Calculation

This is a computer calculation based on actuarial figures to produce income for a spouse based on investments etc and arose in the case of the same name.

Again it will give a starting point but will need adjustment as was shown in *Gojkovic v Gojkovic* (1990).

If periodical payments are to be made the court will look at the source of the money and will look at the effect of the order on that source.

In *Dew v Dew* (1986) using the one-third principle the wife was entitled to £350,000 but as this would have adversely affected the husband's business, the source of the payment, her order was adjusted to £135,000 after full consideration of s 25.

### Property orders
Under s 24 MCA 1973 the court has very wide powers to deal with the property concerned. The problem the court has to deal with is that of providing a spouse and children with the necessary accommodation without taking away the other spouse's interest in the property. This can be done by creating a trust for sale, the sale being suspended until the occurrence of certain events.

### The Mesher order
The wife and children were to occupy the house until the youngest child became 17 years of age or until a further order. The trust for sale

would satisfy both parties interests as on this event occurring the husband would receive his interest in the property.

This type of order, however, has been criticised. It can place the wife onto the housing market at a time when she is financially vulnerable or when the housing market is in a depressed state and her share of the property would be insufficient for her to rehouse herself and her children who may be still at home. It also left the wife financially linked to the husband which goes against the modern trend of ending any ongoing dependence.

### The Martin order

This type of order removed a number of the difficulties resulting from a Mesher order. Here the property is held on a trust for sale by one party during their lifetime or until remarriage or voluntary removal then the results of the sale are fairly distributed. This type of order is much fairer to both sides and is clearly more amenable to the clean break situation as was stated in the case of *Clutton v Clutton* (1991).

### The Harvey order

This is the minor type of order and provides that the spouse retaining the property should, on completion of the mortgage, pay the other spouse an occupational fair rent until the sale is completed and the assets shared.

The courts, in recent years, have also been more in favour of outright transfers of the property with only nominal payments of maintenance being ordered in return for the other spouse's loss of interest. This can suit a clean break situation. However, in a property slump the order for the actual sale of a property may cause difficulties as it may not be sold for its proper value and so will raise insufficient funds to provide homes for both parties. These factors are of importance when considering the orders to be made.

## Section 31 MCA

Under s 31(1) and (2) the court can vary ie increase/reduce, discharge/suspend or revive periodical payments. It also has the power to vary instalments where a lump sum is to be paid in that manner, but only then since it has no power to vary a lump sum paid directly or which is to be paid within a certain time.

When it comes to property the court does have the power to vary an order for the sale of property but does not have the power to vary a property adjustment order. These limitations are placed on the court as lump sum and property adjustment orders are seen as 'once and for all' orders ie the matters are settled so as to allow the parties to know the situation and to plan their future.

When making a decision on variation the court must consider all the circumstances of the case including the facts of the original case as well as any changes that have occurred since *Garner v Garner* (1992). The first consideration is the welfare of any minor child as in s 25. Often applications to vary existing orders arise when financial circumstances change eg a party's income changes and they or the other party think that the order should be varied to reflect these changes. A variation could also be required to meet increased obligations such as increased expenditure for the children as they get older or where a second family has arrived on the scene.

Also in common with s 25A, the 'clean break', the court has to consider whether to vary the order for a limited period under s 31(7). The court's attitude is similar to both situations ie it is often reluctant to apply a clean break. The reluctance in the situation of variation usually shows itself when a party applies for the termination of an order. The court has to consider whether or not the payee would be able to adjust to the new circumstances without undue hardship and a major factor in its judgment would be any future uncertainty. The approach of the courts is often to refuse to terminate the order but to reduce it to a nominal order so that if circumstances were to deteriorate for the payee then she could apply for a further variation and the existence of the nominal order could be seen as a safeguard.

In *Hepburn v Hepburn* (1989) the husband applied for the wife's maintenance to be terminated as she was living with another man. The court was of the opinion that a nominal order should be made rather than a total discharge of the order.

The husband appealed but it was held that cohabitation was not the same as remarriage and the decision to make a nominal order was correct as the wife's relationship with the man could end at any time and the man would have no obligation to maintain the wife whereas the husband did have such an obligation and could afford to fulfil that obligation.

This situation can be compared with *Ashley v Blackman* (1988) where the husband applied for his maintenance order to be discharged as he had remarried, his income was very low, and he now had an obligation to his second wife.

The court considered that s 31(7) was able to deal with situations where parties of limited means could be freed from the burden of ongoing orders and each other. In this case it was felt that the discharge of the order was appropriate as the wife was adequately provided for by state benefits which would only be reduced by similar amounts to those payable by the husband.

It should be remembered that where the parties have agreed on the financial matters, and consent orders have been made the limitations regarding lump sums, property adjustment orders still apply and if a variation of a consent order is sought then it will be necessary to show at least some of the following factors:

- fresh evidence coming to light that was not known at the time the order was made;
- the parties, including the court, relied on erroneous information;
- fraud or non-disclosure which would have led to a substantially different order;
- exceptionally, when the basis for the original order has been destroyed.

In order to avoid these hurdles parties may appeal against an order out of time. However, there are strict limitations on this course of action and leave will only be granted if the applicant can meet the requirements laid down in the case of *Barder v Barder* (1987) which stated that only then would leave be granted.

The requirements are that:

- new events invalidate the basis of the order and an appeal would be likely to succeed; and
- the new event occurred within a few months of the order; and
- the application is made reasonably promptly; and
- the appeal, if granted, would not prejudice third parties who had acted in good faith and for valuable consideration on the basis of the order.

The main reason for such a strict approach is to prevent numerous applications and to maintain certainty in such situations.

The circumstances of this next case are unusually rare and tragic but do illustrate how to apply the correct approach. In the case a consent order was made, part of which required that the husband transfer his halfshare in the home to the wife. Shortly afterwards, about four weeks later, the wife killed their two children before killing herself. On her death her property was to pass to her mother.

The husband applied for leave to appeal out of time since no variation was possible as it was a property adjustment order. The House of Lords granted his application on the basis of the above requirements but said that not every unforeseen change of circumstances will justify such leave being granted.

# Child Support Act 1991

This act came into force on 5 April 1993 and brought an end to the courts ability to make maintenance orders for children defined as 'qualifying children'. This definition is contained in s 8(3) CSA 1991, as a child whose parent(s) are absent from him and who is either under 16 years of age or under 19 years of age and receiving full-time education.

The courts now only have a very limited ability to make maintenance orders for children. They can still make lump sum orders or property orders and can make maintenance orders for step-children who are children of the family since they are not covered by the Act as natural or adopted children are. They can also make orders for disabled children for children from wealthy families where the maintenance deemed necessary exceeds the CSA maximum levels of about £220 per week and can make an order to 'top up' any award. They also have the ability to deal with educational costs not covered by the formulae laid down in the Act.

The CSA 1991 has proved to be a very controversial piece of legislation. The Government's aim in introducing this Act was said to be to ensure that parents fulfil their financial responsibilities towards their children and do not put the burden onto the State. A number of others involved take the view that it is simply a cost-cutting exercise on behalf of the Treasury.

There does seem to be common ground in as much as nearly all parties agree that the basic principle expressed that parents should support their children is correct. However, it is the methods and general approach of the Child Support Agency that has caused much criticism.

## Child Support Agency

This body was set up by the Act to deal with the maintenance of children by absent parents. Applications will be made to the Agency by the parent with care for the child for an order against the absent parent and mathematical formulae are used by child support officers to fix any amount payable. Section 2 CSA 1991 states that the officers must have regard to the welfare of any child likely to be affected by decisions reached by their use of discretionary powers but since the major decisions are based on the formulae any discretion is limited.

The workload of the Agency was expected to be so large that a timetable was laid down for the phasing in over five years from 1993 of the different types of cases involved, commencing with cases that involved new applications for child support and applications from parents with existing maintenance orders who are receiving income support or family credit. It is envisaged that by 1997 all child maintenance orders will be dealt with by the Agency.

### Child Support Act and clean breaks

This has been a major area of concern in the short period the Act has been in operation. Not only has the Act brought about a large increase in the amounts awarded in maintenance orders but parents who thought they had settled such matters along with their divorce have suddenly found that this is not the case.

Clean breaks orders made previously are being altered when former partners are make applications for maintenance assessment. The typical situation is where the husband has given up his interest in the family home in exchange for either only maintenance payments for the children being awarded or only nominal payments, if any, for the wife.

In *Crozier v Crozier* (1993) the husband had transferred his interest in the family home to the wife in settlement of his liability to support her and their child. He was now being required to pay an assessment prepared by the Child Support Agency. He applied for leave to appeal out of time against the clean break consent order.

It was held that the clean break principle was unaffected by both the Child Support Act 1991 and the Social Security Administration Act 1992 under which the husband was being required to provide support as the wife was claiming income support. Applications under these Acts were made by the Secretary of State for Social Security not by the wife.

There have been modifications to the Act recently since there have been claims that Child Support Agency assessments are causing great difficulties and even the breakdown of second marriages but these modifications have been seen as tinkering and of no real improvement to the situation.

## Methods of assessment

These are dealt with only in outline due to their complexity.

There is a set formula laid down in the Act and its attendant regulations for the assessment of the payment to be made by the absent parent. It is based on the Income Support payments in force at a particular time and is made up of the following elements:

- the child's maintenance requirements;
- assessable income of the parent with care AND the absent parent;
- the maintenance assessment.

## The child's maintenance requirement

This is made up of the Income Support payments that would be made to the child and the parent with care but with any Child Benefit payable deducted from the total.

## Assessable incomes

The net income of each parent minus the element of the 'exempt income' ie the income support payment that would be payable or 50% of the income whichever is the greater, is calculated.

## The maintenance assessment

The maintenance assessment is then reached by adding together the assessable incomes of both parents and multiplying the result by 0.5. The result will then determine the amount the absent parent has to contribute. If the result is less than or equal to the child's maintenance requirement then the absent parent will pay half his assessable income. If the result is more than the requirement then a further 25% of income becomes payable up to a maximum amount. This results in wealthier parents being made to pay proportionately more so that their child can benefit from their higher standard of living.

# *Revision Notes*

## Ancillary relief

### Section 23 Matrimonial Causes Act 1973
- Periodical payments end on the death of the payee.
- Secured payments continue after the death of the payee.
- The remarriage or death of the recipient ends both types of payment.

### Section 24 MCA 1973
- Transfer of property.
- *Jones v Jones* (1975).
- Settlement of property.
- Mesher order.
- Martin order.
- Harvey order.
- Variation of settlements.
- Extinction or reduction of an interest in a settlement.

### Section 24A MCA 1973
Express power of sale of any property in which 'either or both spouses has an interest.'

### Section 25(1) MCA 1973
- Welfare of any minor child.
- *Suter v Suter and Jones* (1987).

### Section (2)(a) financial resources
- *Hardy v Hardy* (1981).
- *Newton Newton* (1990).
- New partners.
- *Macey v Macey* (1981).

### Section (2)(b) financial obligations
- Consider the length of future obligations.
- *Mesher v Mesher* (1980).
- *Stockford v Stockford* (1982).

### Section (2)(c) standard of living
- *Calderbank v Calderbank* (1975).
- *Vicary v Vicary* (1992).

### Section (2)(d) ages and duration of the marriage
- *Attar v Attar (No 2)* (1985).
- Cohabitation prior to marriage.
- *H v H* (1981).
- *Kokosinski v Kokosinski* (1980).

### Section (2)(e) disability
- *Jones v Jones* (1975).
- *Seaton v Seaton* (1986).

### Section (2)(f) contributions to the welfare of the family
- Both parties can contribute in different ways.
- Contributions can be positive and negative.
- *Wachtel v Wachtel* (1973).
- *Gojkovic v Gojkovic* (1991).
- *E v E* (1990).

### Section (2)(g) conduct it would be inequitable to disregard
- Court's reluctance to consider.
- Obvious and gross.
- *Wachtel v Wachtel* (1973).
- *Jones v Jones* (1975).
- *Dixon v Dixon* (1974).
- Post divorce conduct.
- *Kyte v Kyte* (1987).

### Section (2)(h) value of any lost benefit
- *Parker vParker* (1972).
- *Julian v Julian* (1972).

### Section 25A MCA 1973
- Court has a duty to consider 'a clean break'.
- *Barratt v Barratt* (1988).
- Need only grant when appropriate.

rare. It must be shown that there is 'real immediate danger of serious injury or incurable damage' before the court will grant an interim order on an ex parte application. Practice Note (Matrimonial Causes: Injunction: ex parte Applications) 1978 and if the other party is readily available for service then it is unlikely to be made. If any form of order is made then it will be strictly limited in time.

# Domestic Proceedings and Magistrates' Court Act 1978

Section 16(1) of this Act allows a spouse to apply to the local magistrates' court to exclude the other spouse from the family home. It does not give such protection to cohabitees.

Section 16(2) allows the court, where satisfied that the respondent has used or threatened to use violence against the person of the applicant or a child of the family and that it is necessary for the protection of the applicant or a child of the family that an order should be made under this subsection, to make one or both of the following orders:

- that the respondent shall not use or threaten to use violence against the person of the applicant;
- that the respondent shall not use or threaten to use violence against the person of a child of the family.

Section 16(3) says that where an application is made under this subsection and the court is satisfied that the respondent has used violence against the applicant or a child of the family; or the respondent has threatened to use violence against the person of the applicant or a child of the family and has used violence against some third person; or that the respondent has in contravention of an order made under subsection (2) threatened to use violence against the person of the applicant or the person of a child of the family, and that the applicant or a child of the family is in danger of being physically injured by the respondent (or would be in such danger if the applicant or child were to enter the matrimonial home) the court may make one or both of the following orders:

- an order requiring the respondent to leave the matrimonial home;
- an order prohibiting the respondent from entering the matrimonial home.

A close reading of the orders show that there is no power to prevent other forms of molestation other than violence to the person of the applicant or a child of the family. Also the classification of child protected is narrower than under the DVMPA where the child is 'a child living with the applicant'.

Under s 16(3) 'the danger of being physically injured' does not have to be an imminent danger but must be an objectively recognisable one. In *McCartney v McCartney* (1981) there had been a number of assaults in the past but there had been no recent incidents and the magistrates decided that there was no danger of physical injury but on appeal it was decided that the danger need not be imminent, a recognisable danger was sufficient.

However, if there is an imminent danger of physical injury the court may make on expedited order forbidding the respondent from using violence. This order lasts for a maximum of 28 days but further orders can be made if the need is shown. The court cannot make such an order excluding the respondent from the home.

When magistrates hear applications for these personal protection orders, as they are often called, and the exclusion orders then they should use the criteria used by the higher courts ie those in s 1(3) MHA to allow consistency throughout the system.

Section 18 DPMCA contains the power to attach a power of arrest to an order but as with the higher courts this should only be used in exceptional circumstances and will only last for a similar length of time. In order for the power to be attached the magistrates must be satisfied that the respondent has physically injured the applicant or a child of the family and is likely to do so again. Note the level of violence required differs under this Act. This power allows a constable to arrest anyone whom he reasonably suspects of being in breach of the order and he must be brought before a magistrate within 24 hours. Due to the draconian nature of the power of arrest it was held in *Widdowson v Widdowson* (1983) the magistrates should give reasons for their decision to attach the power of arrest.

When questions arise on this topic the student will need to consider the availability and suitability of the remedies. The advantages and disadvantages of each measure need to be considered in the light of the particular question and a careful reading of the question is essential as the application and analysis needs to be precise to gain good marks.

## The inherent jurisdiction of the court

If other proceedings are pending between the parties then the High Court and the county court can in certain circumstances grant an injunction to protect the woman. However, this must be in support of an existing legal or equitable right *Ainsbury v Millington* (1986). Also there must be a lack of statutory power covering the situation to enable the court to use this jurisdiction.

In this case the parties who were unmarried were joint tenants of a council flat. After a period of separation the woman married another man and tried to exclude the man from the property.

She was unable to make an application under the MHA since they were unmarried and she was unable to use the DPMCA as they were no longer living together as man and wife in the same household. She made an application under the Supreme Court Act 1981 but the application failed on a number of grounds including the fact that the woman did not have the sole right and so no greater right to occupy the property than the man, and the court will not grant an order where it will merely give one party an advantage over the other in domestic proceedings. It was also deemed to be unnecessary to grant an order to protect the children of the relationship.

In the case of *Franklin v Pearson* (1994) it was stated that in cases that concerned children and the occupation of the matrimonial home, where the parties had been married, the court retained the jurisdiction to grant ouster orders for the protection of the children subject to the criteria laid down in *Richards*. If the parties had never been married then no such jurisdiction existed nor would there be the availability of a s 8 specific issue order under the Children Act. However under s 15 and para 1 of Schedule 1 of that Act rights of ownership and occupation of property can be adjusted for the benefit of the children and once such an application has been made the court can control by injunction the use of the property pending final determination.

Injunctions can also be granted in an action in tort but again only in support of an existing right. In *Patel v Patel* (1988) it was said that there was no tort of harassment and so no injunction could be granted preventing the respondent from going within 50 yards of his father-in-law's house. However, if conduct amounted to another tort, eg trespass, assault or conduct calculated to impair the plaintiff's health and did so then an order could be granted.

In *Burnett v George* (1992) the injunction was upheld on appeal as the court found that there was evidence that the plaintiff's health had been impaired by the respondent's conduct and he was ordered not to assault her or otherwise interfere with her by doing acts calculated to harm her.

Also in the case of *Khorasandjian v Bush* (1993) the Court of Appeal held that there was a tort of harassment and granted an injunction restraining the respondent from harassing, pestering or communicating with the plaintiff by any means. This change in attitude can be seen as filling some of the gaps left by the existing remedies for protection.

## Undertakings

To remove the need for a full hearing and the calling of evidence the party that would otherwise be the subject of the application can agree to give to the court an undertaking that he will not molest the other party and/or will leave the family home as would have been requested by the other party depending on the circumstances of the case.

When such an undertaking is given it will be as binding on the party giving it as if an order had been made by the court (*Hussain v Hussain* (1986)).

## Proposals for reform

As can been seen the present system of law in the area of domestic violence is confused and unsatisfactory when it comes to meeting the needs of today's society. Lord Scarman in *Richards v Richards* (1984) summed up the position when he said:

The statutory provision is a hotchpotch of enactments of limited scope passed into law to meet specific situations or to strengthen the powers of the specified courts. The sooner the range, scope and effect of these powers are rationalised into a coherent and comprehensive body of law the better.

The Law Commission has produced recommendations for reform which are contained in 'Domestic Violence and Occupation of the Family Home', Working Paper No 113, 1989 and 'Family Law: Domestic Violence and Occupation of the Family Home', Law Com No 207, 1992.

The aims of these proposals are to remove the anomalies and inconsistencies of the present system and replace it with a clear, comprehensive and flexible system that will be available in all the courts that have jurisdiction in family matters. At the same time they seek to ensure that there is no reduction in the level of protection available but in fact that there is an improvement and seek to do so by providing effective protection for both adults and children whilst attempting to avoid increasing the tensions that exist between the parties involved.

The existing sources of remedies have been considered but two important areas that are not included in the proposals are those of the aspects of the criminal law relating to domestic violence and those relating to public housing which is often brought into consideration when total breakdown occurs. The latter area is the subject of a Department of the Environment working party.

A draft bill is included in the report and amongst its various measures are selective repeals of existing measures and re-enactments of the best aspects.

A summary of the main points of reform are:

- There would be a single set of remedies available in all the courts dealing with family cases although magistrates' courts would have to refer the more complex and difficult to higher courts.
- There would be non-molestation orders available for a wider range of people including spouses, former spouses cohabitants, former cohabitants, those who live together or have lived together in the same household other than as an employee, tenant or lodger or are within a defined group of close relatives, engaged couples, those who have or have had a sexual relationship (whether or not including sexual intercourse), those who are parents of a child or, in relation to any child are persons who have or have had parental responsibility for that child or they are parties to the same family proceedings.
- A single flexible power to grant orders regulating the occupation of the family home including orders that one person be allowed to occupy or return to or be ordered from that home. In some circumstances the High Court would be able to transfer a tenancy from one party to the other.
- There would be a power of arrest available to all levels of courts where violence has been used or threatened and this would be required to be attached unless the applicant or child will be adequately protected without it. The court should also retain the discretion to grant ex parte orders where it would be just and convenient but only after consideration of certain factors.
- The controversial measure of allowing the police to apply for civil remedies on behalf of the victim if there has been molestation, violence actual or threatened.

However, it is thought that two classes mentioned above will not be included in the reforms when or if they are brought into being. They are:

- people who have at any time agreed to marry each other (whether or not that agreement has been terminated); and
- people who have or have had a sexual relationship with each other (whether or not including sexual intercourse).

It is considered that these groups do not have not the same degree of 'family' link as those in the other groups and would cause difficulties of definition for the courts and their inclusion is not justified.

It has also been recommended by the Home Affairs Select Committee that the proposal that the police be able to take action on behalf of an aggrieved party should also be rejected. This is because they believe that the police would be acting on what would be seen as a 'snapshot' of a particular incident and it would be unreasonable to expect the police to deal with these matters on that basis especially when considering their present resources and level of expertise.

We shall have to wait and see how many of the recommendations will survive the journey to the statute book in their present form, if at all.

This just an outline of the main features of the recommendations.

A careful reading of the papers concerned is necessary since an essay question based on the proposed reforms is likely to occur and the effect of the reforms should be considered so that a balanced argument can be given as to whether or not they have achieved their desired goal.

# *Revision Notes*

## Matrimonial Homes Act 1983

Applications are made in the High Court or the county court.
Orders available (s 1):

- declaring,enforcing,restricting,or terminating rights;
- prohibiting,suspending or restricting the exercise by either spouse of the right to occupy the dwelling house; or
- requiring either spouse to permit the exercise by the other of that right.
  Source of power depends on aspect of ownership.
  Section 1(1). Section 1(11). Section 9.

### Section 1(3) It must be 'just and reasonable' to exclude
Consider:

- conduct of the parties to each other and others;
- their needs and financial resources;
- any children's needs;
- all the circumstances of the case.
  The interests of the children are important but are *not* paramount.
- *Richards v Richards* (1984).
  The draconian nature of an ouster order must be kept in mind when considering s 1(3) and a real need must be shown before an order will be made.

### Weaknesses

- the Act is only available to married couples;
- there is no power of arrest available;
- there is no molestation order available;

Consider an application under both the Matrimonial Homes Act and the Domestic Violence and Matrimonial Proceedings Act 1976 to overcome the weaknesses.

Domestic Violence and Matrimonial Proceedings Act 1976.

Applications are usually made in the county court.

Orders may be made after consideration of the factors in s 1(3).

## MHA

Orders available:
- a molestation order for the applicant and/or a child living with the applicant;
- an order excluding the other party from the home and the surrounding area;
- an order requiring the other party to allow the applicant to occupy the home.

Note the class of child protected.

### Molestation
Its definition and types of behaviour covered.
- *F v F* (1989).
- *Johnson v Walton* (1990).

### Section 2(1) a power of arrest is available
- Actual bodily harm and likely to do so again.
- *Kendrick v Kendrick* (1990).

### Section 1(2) DVMPA makes the orders available to both married and unmarried couples
- Domestic Proceedings and Magistrates' Courts Act 1978.
- Applications are made to the magistrates' court.
- Orders must be shown to be necessary to provide protection and violence has been used or threatened.

Orders available:
- that the respondent shall not use or threaten violence against the applicant;
- that the respondent shall not use or threaten violence against the child.

Note the class of child protected.

Where the court is satisfied that the respondent has used or threatened violence and has used violence against a third party or is in breach of one of the above orders it may make one or both of the following orders:
- to require the respondent to leave the home; and/or
- to prohibit the respondent from entering the home.

### Section 18 a power of arrest is available
- Physical injury and likely to do so again.
- Need not be imminent danger.

- *McCartney v McCartney* (1981).
- The Act is available only to married couples.

## Proposals for reform

- Law Commission Working Paper No 113 1989.
- Law Commission Working Paper No 207 1992.

### Aims

To overcome the defects in the present system by providing consistent, flexible remedies, increase protection whilst reducing tension between the parties.

## Summary of recommendations

- Single set of remedies at all levels of court.
- Increase the groups of people to be protected.
- Single power of occupation.
- New attitude towards the power of arrest.
- Police powers - if retained.

# 6 Children

Children are the product of most relationships between men and women and on their arrival the difficult task of bringing them up arises for the parents. There have been different attitudes towards this task and society's views have changed over the years. Parents have had, at different times, different levels of control and responsibility towards their children.

These have varied from the father being in total control of the family including the mother and making decisions that suited his needs with little or no thought for others and allowed him to treat the other family members as chattels to today's position where marriage is seen as a partnership and the parents should do what is in the best interests of their children.

An important case that illustrates such change in attitude is *Gillick v West Norfolk and Wisbech AHA* (1985).

The case concerned a mother a staunch Catholic who objected to a circular that had been issued by the Department of Health and Social Security to doctors advising them that they were able in certain circumstances to prescribe contraceptives to children under 16 years of age without parental consent.

Mrs Gillick sought a declaration that the circular was illegal and interfered with her parental rights as she held firm religious beliefs against such medical advice and treatment.

It was decided in this landmark case that although parents did obviously have a say in the way that their children were brought up and they did have rights over their children's lives these rights arose from the duties they owed the children and were there to provide any necessary protection the child may need and as the need for protection diminished so did the rights of the parents.

This case brought into being the concept of the 'Gillick competent' child which will be seen as an important development which has been enlarged by the Children Act 1989.

The Family Law Reform Act 1969 had given young people over the age of 16 the statutory right to consent to medical treatment but there was no legal guidance as to the extent of parental rights over children under 16 who required medical advice as was the case in *Gillick*. In any case, regarding the extent of parental rights matters had to be decided in the light of what was best for the child and this could vary with the child's age and understanding and that a child with sufficient maturity could be allowed to make his own decisions although it will be seen later in this chapter that even though this is now generally accepted there will be times when the court will still overrule children normally seen as 'Gillick competent' in exceptional circumstances usually medical cases.

Parents whether married or not do have duties and responsibilities towards their children. They include amongst others the duty to care for the child's physical well-being and failure to do so could result in criminal liability if it can be shown that they did so deliberately or recklessly. In *R v Shepherd* (1981) the parents were acquitted as they were seen to be of low intellect and unable to appreciate the true situation when the child died of hypothermia and malnutrition.

They also have the duty to ensure that their children are educated under the Education Act 1944 and failure to do so could lead to the prosecution of the parents and in extreme cases could lead to the child being taken into the care of the local authority. There is also a duty on the parents to financially maintain their children that arises under not only under common law but also under the Social Security Administration Acts as well as other legislation.

The latest attitude towards what is expected of parents is shown by the concept of parental responsibility contained in the Children Act 1989.

The definition is contained in s 3(1):

In this Act "parental responsibility" means all the rights, duties, powers, responsibilities and authority which by law a parent of a child has in relation to the child and his property.

This definition is seemingly wide ranging but is vague and does not grant any absolute rights to parents over their children. The position is still similar to that with 'Gillick competent' children in as much as a great deal depends on the age and understanding of the child concerned although under the Children Act, as we shall see, the wishes and feelings of the child are included in the s 1(3) checklist and will be considered by the court, again in the light of their age and understanding, when deciding on whether to grant certain orders. Where young children are involved, the parents will have a greater degree of responsibility to protect the child whereas as the child grows older they will have a diminishing level of responsibility and this lessens to just a duty to advise the child as he approaches maturity as was stated in *Hewer v Bryant* (1969).

Parental responsibility is granted equally to both parents if they are married but only to the mother if she is unmarried. The unmarried father is still a 'parent' under the Act but must take certain steps if he wishes to acquire parental responsibility. He can negotiate with the mother and they can make a 'parental responsibility' agreement which to be effective must be drawn up in the proper form or he can apply to the court for an order granting him parental responsibility under s 4 of the Act.

Those with parental responsibility are usually the parents but can be other people who could gain parental responsibility by being granted a Residence Order. Each such person has the right to act independently of the others in the best interests of the child and the others can only interfere with those actions in limited circumstances eg where the consent of all those with parental responsibility is required to allow adoption or where the actions are in contravention of a court order.

Parental responsibility cannot be given away. The parents will retain it even if they divorce, if the child is made the subject of a care order they will share it with the local authority and they cannot transfer it to another party in an attempt to avoid their responsibilities. Parental responsibility can be brought to an end by the child being adopted resulting in the parental responsibility being vested in the adoptive parents on the child reaching maturity, marrying or joining the armed forces.

## Children Act 1989

The Children Act 1989 came into effect on 14 October 1991 and has been recognised as the most important piece of legislation concerning children this century. It shows the changing attitudes of society and has brought about wide-ranging changes in the whole area whether it be in private law or public law matters. The need for change had been recognised for a number of years. Working parties had reported and recommended changes and these along with a number of tragic events such as the deaths of Jasmine Beckford and Kimberley Carlisle and the subsequent reports combined with the Cleveland Report on child abuse helped to bring about some of the improvements contained in the Act.

The Act introduces a new philosophy of non-intervention by the state in the affairs of the family unless it is deemed necessary to protect the children from suffering significant harm and even if any action is deemed necessary then if possible the action should be taken whilst the child remains within the family. An important aim of the Act is to provide a flexible, consistent set of remedies and orders that would be available at all levels of the legal system and to make them available whether the matter be one of private or public law. This attempt at unification of both areas of law has been largely successful and has provided much of the sought-after flexibility.

The Act has achieved this by introducing certain principles which generally apply in situations where the court determines a question concerning the welfare of a child. These principles are contained in s 1 of the Act.

- s 1(1) – the welfare principle – the welfare of the child is paramount.
- s 1(2) – the delay principle – there should be no delay in proceedings as it may affect the child's welfare.
- s 1(3) – the checklist – the factors to be considered when dealing with applications that are considered to be within the definition of 'family proceedings' contained in s 8(3)(4) of the Act and the circumstances contained in s 1(4) arise.
- s 1(5) – the 'no order principle' – that the court should make no order unless a benefit can be seen to arise for the child from the granting of the order.

The absolutely fundamental importance of these principles must be appreciated as they form the basis of the court's decision. This can be seen in situations such as applications for care orders where even when the necessary criteria for the granting of such orders have been fulfilled the court will consider the contents of s 1 prior to the granting of such an order.

Section 1(1) – the welfare principle – is the foundation stone of the new philosophy contained in the Act and in most matters dealt with by the Act the welfare of the child is paramount.

However, there are instances when the welfare principle will only be applied at certain times. Such an instance is during child protection proceedings. After the necessary criteria have been shown to exist only then will the court consider the child's welfare. However, it must be borne in mind that this principle does not necessarily apply in other areas of law not covered by the Children Act eg adoption, applications under the Matrimonial Homes Act 1983 and divorce. In these proceedings the child's welfare is seen as a very important factor to be considered when reaching a decision but it will not be seen as paramount.

Section 1(2) provides that the court must have regard to the fact that delay in proceedings regarding the upbringing of the child may have a prejudicial effect on the welfare of the child. This has led to the requirement contained in s 11 that the court draw up a timetable with a view to determine such questions without delay and to give such directions as are considered appropriate to ensure that the timetable is followed.

This does not necessarily mean that all delay will be seen as being against the welfare of the child. Some delays will be seen as beneficial to the determination of the case such as when a full social report can be given to the court as opposed to a short outline of the family background.

In the case of *C v Solihull MBC* (1993) it was stated 'that planned and purposeful delay may well be beneficial. A delay of a final decision for the purpose of ascertaining the result of an assessment is proper delay and is to be encouraged'.

Section 1(3) contains what has become commonly known as the 'checklist' and contains the factors that the court is required to consider when dealing with the circumstances mentioned in s 1(4), ie:

- the court is considering whether to make vary or discharge a s 8 order and the making, variation or discharge of the order is opposed by any party to the proceedings; or
- the court is considering whether to make vary or discharge an order under Part IV.

Note the fact that there will be opposition to the application.
The factors to be considered are:

- the ascertainable wishes and feeling of the child concerned (considered in the light of his age and understanding);
- his physical, emotional and educational needs;
- the likely effect on him of any change in his circumstances;

- his age, sex, background and any characteristic of his which the court considers relevant;
- any harm which he has suffered or is at risk of suffering;
- how capable each of his parents and any other person in relation to whom the court considers the question to be relevant is of meeting his needs;
- the range of powers available to the court under the Act in the proceedings in question.

The first item on the checklist is another example of the change in attitude towards children. Although the Act does not give the factor more weight than any of the others it could be seen that its position at the head of the list could give it added significance and there is little doubt that increasing importance will be given to the views expressed by children. However, it must be remembered this will be in the light of their age and understanding. This was the position in the case of *M v M* (1992) where the views of the children who were aged 11 and 10 had been given insufficient consideration and on appeal orders were made reflecting their views.

Where there is conflict regarding the making of a s 8 order then following Practice Direction (Family Division: Conciliation) 1992 the matter will be referred to a welfare officer who will confer privately with the parties in an attempt to reach agreement. It has been directed that children aged nine years or over should be present at such discussions and younger children may also be present. This indicates that the views of even relatively young children should be given some credence. It must be borne in mind that parents can sometimes exercise undue influence over their children's views and the court should try and ensure that the views the children express are their own and not those of persuasive parents.

Section 1(5) illustrates the basis of the philosophy underlying the Act. This is one of the most influential principles contained in the Act, ie the principle of non-intervention by the State in the family. It provides:

... where a court is considering whether or not to make one or more orders under this Act with respect to a child, it shall not make that order or any of the orders unless it considers that doing so would be better for the child than making no order at all.

In *B v B (Grandparent: Residence Order)* 1992. Section 1(5) was considered and the justices hearing the case decided in light of s 1(5) that no residence order was to be made in favour of the grandmother with whom the child was living since they could see no benefit for the child. On appeal the decision was reversed and an order was granted. It was held that without the order the grandmother had no status as far as the education authority was concerned and could not give consent for such everyday matters as school trips or in more extreme circumstances could not give consent for medical treatment and the mother of the child could remove her at any moment. A residence order granted to the grandmother would relieve these difficulties by giving her parental responsibility automatically which would allow her to act in the interests of the child's welfare and in this case would clearly be to the benefit of the child.

The importance of these basic principles cannot be overestimated. It must be appreciated that they form the basis of the courts' decisions and it will be seen that even in matters such as the granting of care orders they will be considered even when the criteria for the granting of the care order has been met. It will not necessarily follow that the order will be made unless to do so is deemed to be necessary on consideration of the matters contained in s 1.

## The new orders

An important aim of the Act was to introduce a new range of orders which would provide courts at all levels with a flexibility that would enable them to deal with matters occurring across the spectrum of family law matters be they private or public law matters. These new orders are contained in s 8 of Part II of the Act and, not surprisingly, have become known collectively as 'section 8 orders'.

The orders are:

- residence orders, contact orders, prohibited steps orders and specific issues orders.

Section 10(1) of the Act gives the court the power to make s 8 orders in any family proceedings in which a question arises with respect to the welfare of any child if:

- an application for the order has been made by a person who:
  (a) is entitled to apply for a s 8 order with respect to the child; or
  (b) has obtained the leave of the court to make the application; or
- the court considers that the order should be made even though no such application has been made.

The first point of note is 'What are family proceedings?' The definition is contained in s 8(3) and (4).

**Section 8(3):**
For the purposes of this Act 'family proceedings' means any proceedings:

(a)   under the inherent jurisdiction of the High Court in relation to children; and
(b)   under the enactments mentioned in subsection (4), but does not include proceedings on an application for leave under s 100(3).

**Section 8(4):**
The enactments are:

(a)  Parts I, II, and IV of this Act;
(b)  the Matrimonial Causes Act 1973;
(c)  the Domestic Violence and Matrimonial Proceedings Act 1976;
(d)  the Adoption Act 1976;
(e)  the Domestic Proceedings and Magistrates' Courts Act 1978;
(f)  ss 1 and 9 of the Matrimonial Homes Act 1983;
(g)  Part III of the Matrimonial and Family Proceedings Act 1984.

## Residence orders

Residence orders settle the arrangements to be made as to the person with whom the child is to live.

A residence order most frequently occurs in family breakdown situations and is used to settle disputes over what was previously known as custody. The intention behind the order is not just to decide who has possession of the child, it will also mean they take on the everyday responsibilities of care for the child. Because of this, the matter of parental responsibility must be considered because as to fulfil this task the person with the residence order must be able to take everyday decisions regarding the upbringing of the child. If it is granted to a married parent then it will not alter the situation that each parent will retain parental responsibility and each is able to act independently for the benefit of the child. If the order is granted to an unmarried father then the court is obliged to grant him parental responsibility by way of a s 4 'parental responsibility order' (s 12(1)) and he will share it with the mother.

If the order is granted to a non-parent then they will be granted parental responsibility (s 12(2) which they will share with the parent but it will be limited in as much as the non-parent will be unable to consent to or refuse to consent to an adoption or appoint a guardian (s 12(3)).

A residence order is the only s 8 order that can be made if the child is in the care of the local authority (s 9(1)). If it is granted then it will bring the care order to an end (s 91(1)) and it should be remembered that a local authority cannot apply for or be granted a residence order (s 9(2)).

A matter which crops up in some questions is that of joint residence orders ie an order which will allow the child to share his time between both parents eg spending school time with mother and holiday time with father. The case of *Riley v Riley* (1986) frowned on the practice but can no longer be regarded as good law as s 11(4) allows a residence order to be made in favour of two or more persons who do not themselves live together and may specify the periods that the child can spend in the different households. In *A v A (children: shared residence order)* (1994) it was stated that joint residence orders should only be made in unusual circumstances. The court should consider whether there was anything of positive value to the child on consideration of the criteria in s 1 of the Act and should not make such an order unless there was agreement between the parents as to the actual arrangements.

Section 11(5) goes on to say that if a joint residence order is granted to one of two parents with parental responsibility and the parents live together for a continuous period of more than six months then the residence order will cease to have effect.

When there is a contested residence order hearing the court will obviously consider s 1(3), the first item being the wishes and feelings of the child. In *B v B (Minors) (Residence and Care Disputes)* (1994) guidelines were laid down as to how judges should use their discretion in interviewing a child in private. It was said that the judge should have good reason to see the child and it would be in his interests to be seen. The child should be seen after submissions by the parties but before the closing speeches so his opinion could be better valued by the judge, but he had to be made aware that there could be no confidentiality of the child's views from the parents and, even though the judge would consider the child's views to be important, the final decision would be that of the court and may vary from the wishes of the child due to s 1(1). If this was the case then it had to be made clear to the child that he bore no responsibility or blame for the decision.

Following the granting of a residence order the contents of s 13 of the Act must be considered. It states that if such an order is in force then no person may:

- cause the child to be known by a new surname; or
- remove him from the UK;

without the written consent of every person who has parental responsibility for the child or the leave of the court.

The latter provision is tempered to some degree by the fact that a child can be taken out of the country for a period of less than one month by the person in whose favour the residence order is made. This is seen as being a practical approach since otherwise consent would need to be sought on a regular basis just for family holidays abroad.

The court will reach it's decision on the matter of a change of surname by following the principles laid down in *W v A (Child: Surname)* (1981). In this case it was said that changing a child's name was not a matter to be taken lightly and would normally only be permissible if it could be shown that it would be in the child's interests. This approach was confirmed in the recent case of *Re F (Child: Surname)* (1993) where the mother had applied for her daughters to be known by her maiden name. The father appealed against the granting of the order and it was stated that appeal should be allowed as the judge had failed to follow the principles in *W v A* and had failed to consider whether there was any need or significant benefit for the children by allowing the change.

Again when considering whether to grant leave for the child to leave the country the court must bear in mind the contents of s 1, ie the welfare principle, the checklist and the 'no order' principle. The cases that occur in this area are often concerning a family that wishes to emigrate with the child. A useful comparison can be made between *M v A (Wardship: Removal from Jurisdiction)* (1993) and *Re B (Minors) (Removal from Jurisdiction)* (1994). In the former case the parents of the two children aged 12 and 9 had separated but lived close to each other and the children retained close contact with their father whilst living with the mother. The mother applied for leave to remove the children to Canada, her home country. Leave was refused as the children did not wish to leave the country and the mother had not planned their new life to a sufficient degree as she had no job to go to and there was no schooling arranged for the children.

In the latter case the two children aged 12 and 10 did not have any great degree of contact with their father and their mother and her new husband applied to move France. She undertook to allow the children to return to England to visit their father. The judge was of the opinion that the children's welfare would be best served by granting leave. The father's appeal failed since it was considered that there would be resentment felt by the children if the order had been refused and that would adversely affect the relationship between the father and the children.

Both these elements show that even if only one parent is awarded a residence order the other parent still has continuing parental responsibility and any relationship that exists between the non-resident parent and the child will be protected at least to some extent. Remember these restrictions come into being after the making of a residence order and do not apply until then.

## Contact orders

This an order requiring the person with whom the child lives or is to live to allow the child to visit or to stay with the person named in the order or for that and the child otherwise to have contact with each other.

The order covers the area formerly known as access. It allows the non-resident parent or any other person named in the order to retain contact with the child in a way to be decided by the court. This could be by stays, visits, letters or telephone calls depending on the circumstances of the case.

It has been stated in the case of *M v M* (1973) that the right to contact is to be regarded as a right of the *child* not of the parent or whoever is seeking contact. When reaching its decision on the matter of contact the court must bear in mind that the paramount consideration is the welfare of the child and if there is conflict between the parties then the s 1(3) checklist must also be borne in mind. This is frequently the case as these orders are usually sought in cases of family breakdown and bitterness and resentment can lead to a failure to reach an amicable agreement.

The accepted approach to the subject of contact is that there is a presumption that the child will benefit by retaining contact with both parents and contact should be allowed unless it can be shown to be detrimental to the child's welfare as was illustrated in *Re H (Minors) (Access)* (1992) where on appeal it was felt that the children would, in the long-term, benefit from continued contact with the father even though there had been some time since they had last had contact with him.

If there is a contested application for contact then it is a matter for the court to decide on s 1 considerations. The parents' attitude towards each other on the matter of contact can be an indication to the court of their true attitude regarding the child's welfare, ie if they allow their hostility towards each other to affect their judgment as to what is best for the child's welfare. In *D v M ( A Minor: Custody Appeal)* (1982) the father's opposition to allowing the mother contact with the child was seen as a factor that weighed against him when the court balanced the circumstances of the case.

In *Re J (A Minor) (Contact)* (1994) it was said that the court should be reluctant to allow the hostility of a party with a residence order to deter them from making a contact order in favour of another party if it was shown that to make the order would be in the child's welfare.

In extreme cases it has been held that the court has the power not only to strike out an application for a consent order but also to direct that no further application be made for a period of time. In *Re T (A Minor) (Parental Responsibility: Contact)* (1993) the unmarried father of the child sought the orders for the child after his relationship with the mother had broken down and had deteriorated into violence on a number of occasions. At one time he had been granted limited access and had failed to keep to the terms of that order by keeping the child for nine days. He had also failed to follow the conditions of a maintenance order for the child. This led to the orders being terminated. The father applied for parental responsibility and for a change of the child's surname. The applications were dismissed on the ground that he had treated the mother with hostility and violence and had shown disregard for the welfare of the child.

He then applied for a variation of the order terminating his access but an order was made under the inherent jurisdiction of the court and s 91(14) of the Children Act that there should be no application by the father for any s 8 order for three years.

It was said that such an order was unusual and should be used sparingly. However, in this case, it was felt that contact with the father would endanger the child's welfare and the order was justified.

Under usual circumstances it will be seen that a contact order will be granted to allow contact between the child and the non-resident parent but the problem has arisen of whether or not a contact order can be made ordering that there be no contact between them. Although there is still some discussion as to whether or not it is the correct approach to the problem in the case of *Nottinghamshire County Council v P (No 2)* (1993)it was held that such an order could be made.

Section 11(7) allows the court to attach directions as to how s 8 orders are to be carried out and can attach conditions.

This power can be used in cases where, for example, contact is seen as being in the child's interests but there may be a need for such contact to be supervised. Such a need could arise where there are allegations of abuse against a parent of the child which are being investigated but to prevent contact prior to the matter being settled could adversely affect the child. The court may then direct that contact should take place under the supervision of an appropriate person such as a social worker.

The usual way such an order would be effected would be by way of a family assistance order under s 16 of the Children Act which would allow a social worker from the local authority to be allocated to advise assist and befriend any person named in the order, thus allowing supervision. This was illustrated in the case of *Re DH (A Minor) (Child Abuse)* (1994) where although such a step was not found to be necessary because of the availability of a supervision order it was stated that neither s 11(7) nor a specific issues order would be the appropriate way to achieve the required result.

Contact by way of a contact order under s 8 of the Children Act should not be confused with contact by way of s 34 of the Act. Under s 34 there is a presumption that contact with the parents will be allowed whilst the child is in care, whilst some think it odd that no such presumption is made when considering s 8 contact orders. Unlike a residence order, a contact order cannot be made if the child is in the care of a local authority.

Residence orders and contact orders are considered to be the primary orders contained in s 8 of the Act. Prohibited steps orders and specific issues orders are seen as secondary orders as is illustrated by the restrictions placed on their use by s 9(5).

Because of this subsection the court cannot exercise its power to make either order with a view to achieving a result which could be achieved by making a residence order or a contact order or in any way which is denied to the High Court (by s 100(2)) in the exercise if its inherent jurisdiction with respect to children. It is said that it prevents the use of such orders to gain certain aims via 'the back door' approach and ensures that the primary orders and inherent jurisdiction are used in the appropriate circumstances.

In *Nottinghamshire County Council v P* (1993) it was held that a prohibited steps order that prevented contact between the father and the children and excluded him from the family home could not be allowed to stand as it was seen as achieving a result that could be achieved by the making of a residence order or a contact order and the local authority was attempting to use the 'back door' approach to the problem.

## Prohibited steps orders

These are defined in the Act as 'an order that no step which could be taken by a parent in meeting his parental responsibility for a child and which is of the kind specified in the order shall be taken by any person without the consent of the court.

It will be seen that the order covers steps that fall within the area of parental responsibility and so is to some extent limited in its application in as much as it cannot to be used to prevent steps that would not come within this ambit, eg assault or molestation and other measures would be needed in those circumstances.

The definition of parental responsibility is contained in s 3(1) of the Act but does not lay down an exhaustive list of duties. As we have seen it will depend on the child involved and his age and understanding. This type of order is meant to deal with individual or single issues in a particular case and is meant to prevent a particular step being taken. A common example would be an order preventing the removal of a child from the UK in a case where there was no residence order in force and so no prohibition under s 13 to prevent such removal.

Normally such an order would be made against one of the parents of the child who can, as we have seen, exercise his responsibility alone provided it is not incompatible with a court order. However, this order can be made against 'any person'. A person that could be named in the order could be any person that could take a step that could be taken via parental responsibility. This could include a teacher or an unmarried father who does not have parental responsibility and could be prevented from consenting to medical treatment for the child.

## Specific issues orders

This is defined as:

an order giving a direction for the purpose of determining a specific question which has arisen or which may arise in connection with any aspect of parental responsibility for a child.

Again it will be seen that it is to deal with normally a single issue and so is similar to a prohibited steps order and is also limited by the matter being within the area of parental responsibility. Where there is a dispute between the parents on a specific matter the court can resolve the matter by granting this type of order and stating the necessary course of action. Such an area of conflict could be the issue of a child's education as was the case in *Re P (A Minor) (Education)* (1992). There was a dispute as to whether or not a child should continue at a public boarding school or transfer to a local day school. This case illustrates that the court will decide the matter on the factors contained in s 1 of the Act and that this will include the child's wishes which would be considered by the court but not necessarily followed. In this case the father appealed against a refusal to vary an order that his son attend the public school as he said he could no longer afford the fees and that the boy no longer wished to attend that school. It was said that this was a difficult case but that the boy's wishes tipped the balance. The boy was 14 at the time and was seen to appreciate his situation and the court paid due respect to his views.

It is clear that the matter was covered by parental responsibility and as such a specific issue order was the proper way to deal with the dispute.

Another important case involving the granting of a specific issues order was *Re HG (Specific Issue: Procedure)* (1993) where it was held that as there was an element of parental responsibility present in deciding the question of the child's treatment then the availability of a specific issue order was beyond question. The procedure for deciding such questions was also laid down for use in future cases.

## Who can apply for s 8 orders ?

### Section 10(4):
The following persons are entitled to apply to the court for any s 8 order with respect to a child:

(a)   any parent or guardian of the child;
(b)   any person in whose favour a residence order is in force with respect to the child.

These parties do not require leave to apply for an order and it should be remembered that an unmarried father is included in this group.

### Section 10(5):
The following persons are entitled to apply for a residence or contact order with respect to the child:

(a)   any party to a marriage (whether or not subsisting) in relation to whom the child is a child of the family;

(b)   any person with whom the child has lived for a period of at least three years;

(c)   any person who:
   (i)   in any case where a residence order is in force with respect to the child has the consent of each of the persons in whose favour the order was made;
   (ii)   in any case where the child is in the care of the local authority has the consent of that authority;
   (iii) in any other case has the consent of each of those (if any) who have parental responsibility for the child.

The persons in this group are seen as the type of applicant that would not normally encounter difficulty when applying for residence or contact orders and it is considered that no hurdles should be put in their way. Their use of prohibited steps and specific issue orders would be seen as out of the ordinary and as such they will require leave to apply for such orders.

An example of the flexibility brought into the area of remedies available under the Children Act is that fact that any person can apply for a s 8 order. If they are not included in the above groups then they must apply to the court for leave to apply for an order (s 10(a)(ii)).

The factors the court has to consider when dealing with an application for leave are contained in s 10(9):

(a)   the nature of the proposed application for the s 8 order;

(b)   the applicant's connection with the child;

(c)   any risk there might be of that proposed application disrupting the child's life to such an extent that he would be harmed by it; and

(d)   where the child is being looked after by a local authority –
   (i)   the authority's plans for the child's future and the wishes and feelings of the child's parents.

A point of importance that must be remembered is that the welfare of the child is not paramount when the matter of leave is being considered by the court (*Re A and W (Minors) (Residence Order: Leave to Apply)* (1992)). It is felt that the correct time to consider the matter of the child's welfare is at the full hearing when the full merits of the case can be considered and not at the leave stage.

A problem that could arise in cases where the child has been in foster care is contained in s 9(3). Where the child is, or has been, at any time within the last six months, in foster care then the person who had care of the child, ie the foster parent, may not apply for leave to apply for a s 8 order unless:

- he has the consent of the authority;
- he is a relative of the child; or
- the child has lived with him for at least three years preceding the application.

The time period mentioned in this restriction need not be continuous but must have not begun more than five years before the making of the application.

## When can children apply for s 8 orders?

Students must bear in mind that in problem questions it may be necessary to consider whether or not the child needing advice may well be able to help himself by applying for a s 8 order.

If the question does arise then the child must apply for leave to apply for such an order and the court in order to grant leave must be satisfied that the child has sufficient understanding to make the proposed application. This will obviously be judged on the age and maturity of the particular child involved in each case and because of the difficulties that arise in such case such applications should be heard by the High Court (Practice Direction 1993).

A useful case to consider is *Re SC (A Minor) (Child's Wishes)* (1993). In this case the child was aged 14 and, having lived in care for eight years, she applied for leave to apply for a residence order to allow her to live with a family friend rather than at home. Her mother opposed the application.

The court was satisfied that she had the understanding necessary to make the application but that did not necessarily mean that the application would succeed. The court also had to bear in mind the chances of success and did not have the benefit of the guidance available under s 10(9) to reach its decision.

## Family assistance order

A new type of order introduced by the Children Act is the Family Assistance order contained in s 16 of the Act.

In family proceedings the court can make a family assistance requiring either a probation officer or a local authority officer, usually a social worker, to be made available to advise, assist and befriend any person named in the order. However, before the order can be made the local authority must agree to making the officer available (s 16(7)).

The persons that can be named in the order are those mentioned in s 16(2) they are:

- the child himself;
- the parent or guardian of the child;
- any person with whom the child is living or who has a contact order in his favour with respect to the child.

These persons, with the exception of the child, who are named in the order are also required to consent to the order being made (s 16(3)). The order can only be made for a maximum of six months and will only be available in exceptional circumstances.

The type of situation that this order could be of use is where there is a need for supervised contact as mentioned above or where the parents need the help of the local authority to assist them during a short period of difficulty until they can find their feet once more.

This order will only be made by the court on its own motion and no applications can be made for this type of order.

## Private law

### Family breakdown

The breakdown in family relationships is becoming ever-more frequent in today's society and this is so whether or not the parties are married. This in turn leads to more difficulties for children as the effects of family breakdown can lead to them having feelings of guilt and anger, problems at school and in extreme cases even becoming involved in crime.

The law recognises that it has a duty to do something to try and avoid the adverse affects that such difficulties have on children's lives when they are involved in such situations through no choice of their own.

One way in which this can be attempted is to allow the parties involved to settle matters between themselves without undue bitterness and hostility and the increased use of mediation could lead to an improvement in this area. However, because of human nature it seems that no matter what improvements or reforms are put in place there are bound to be cases where the parties will fail to agree on matters concerning their children and will have to resort to the law to settle the dispute. The usual way is now via the orders in s 8 of the Children Act 1989 as the most frequent disputes concern where the child is going to live and with whom he is going to have contact.

Where the parents are married they will both have parental responsibility and this will continue after divorce along with their other obligations towards the child. Their ability to meet these obligations will depend on the outcome of the ancillary relief awarded by the court. We have seen that such matters are decided by the court by consideration of the factors contained in s 25 MCA 1973. Section 25(1) says that the first consideration should be given to the welfare of any child of the family.

It must be remembered that it is the *first* consideration not the paramount consideration as in the Children Act.

Along with this factor is the measure contained in s 41(1) MCA 1973 (as amended by Schedule 12 para 31 Children Act 1989) which states that in cases of divorce, nullity and judicial separation the court must consider:

- whether there are any children of the family to this which section applies; and
- where there are any such children, whether (in the light of the arrangements which have been, or are proposed to be made, for their upbringing and welfare) it should exercise any of it powers under the Children Act 1989 with respect to any of them.

This illustrates that the initial responsibility for these arrangements remains with the parents and that the court only has a supervisory duty to ensure that they are satisfactory. This an example of the non-interventionist philosophy of the Children Act.

Section 41(2) gives the court the power to direct that the final decree should not be granted until it is satisfied with the arrangements or the court can direct that further evidence can be filed before the court or seek a welfare report or order the parents to report the court.

Section 41 provides a degree of protection by ensuring that the court has a duty to look at the arrangements for the children but it does not settle the disputes or assist in doing so other than by making sure that the parents have at least thought about them.

The orders that are available to settle these disputes are contained in s 8 of the Children Act and their nature has been discussed above. The most usual types of orders sought are for residence and contact.

When making orders in this area the court will base its decision on the principles contained in s 1 of the Children Act with, of course, the child's welfare being paramount. However the s 1(3) 'checklist' as it has become known must be considered by the court and although it is not an exhaustive list it does contain the major factors that will occur in the majority of cases but the court has the ability to consider all relevant factors.

**Section 1(3):**
(a)    the ascertainable wishes and feelings of the child concerned (considered in the light of his age and understanding;
(b)    his physical emotional and educational needs;
(c)    the likely effect on him of any change in his circumstances;
(d)    his age sex background and any other characteristics of his which the court considers relevant;
(e)    any harm which he has suffered or is at risk of suffering;
(f)    how capable each of his parents and any other person in relation to whom the court considers the question to be relevant is of meeting his needs;
(g)    the range of powers available to the court under this Act in the proceedings in question.

## The ascertainable wishes and feelings of the child

This factor develops the philosophy of 'Gillick' competence and the child's wishes will be judged in the light of his age and understanding, ie that of the particular child involved in the case. No hard and fast rule can be applied in these cases as the ability of each child as an individual must be assessed.

One general approach that can be adopted is that if the child is of or is near to teenage then usually the court will give his opinion some credence but if younger then the court will treat his view with caution. This can be illustrated by the decision in *M v M* (1992).

This factor does not carry priority over the other factors in s 1(3) but its position at the head of the list can be seen as a change in attitude towards children's views.

Also if other things are seen as being equal then the child's views could be the decisive factor but the court will try and ensure that the views expressed by the child are his own and not those of the parent who has exercised influence over the child as in *Re P (Minors) (Wardship: Care and Control)* (1992).

## The child's physical emotional and educational needs

The child's physical needs obviously include the family home and the overall care provided by the parents. The court will also take an overall view of the situation and look at the child's happiness which will depend on a number of factors.

His emotional needs are specifically mentioned as the child's real welfare is best served when the child is happily settled and does not depend solely on being materially well-off.

This can mean that as long as one parent is able to provide an adequate home and care then they will not necessarily lose out to the other partner who may be better-off.

Although it is often thought that the court will almost automatically make an order in favour of the mother a study of the case law will show that this is not so and the correct approach for the court is to treat the factor of babies or young children remaining with the mother as a consideration not a presumption as was stated in *Re S (A Minor) (Custody)* (1991). However it will be difficult to displace this consideration if all other thing are seen as equal (*Re A (A Minor) (Custody)* (1991)).

The make-up of the family unit can also be an important factor and as significant damage has already be caused to the unit by the loss of a parent it could be important to try and keep the other family members together as far as possible especially when siblings are involved. This can be particularly important if they are close in age. However, this factor does lose some effect if there is a large age gap between the children.

Another consideration to be borne in mind is that of the child's educational needs. This factor could cover not only the scholastic potential of the child but also his relationships and friendships at school which if adversely affected could harm his long-term prospects.

The continuity of care being provided for the child is also an important factor. The parent that can provide care for the child without having to use other people as babysitters or causing the child to have to travel from place to place to be cared for will be seen to have an advantage over the other when seeking an order as can be seen in the case of *Re K (Minors) (Care and Control)* (1977). In this case even though it had been found that the wife had committed adultery and the father, a clergyman, was seen as of good character the wife was granted the order as she was able to provide continuity of care whereas the father would have to arrange for a number of other people to care for the children.

Some of the difficulties that may arise in this area could now be diminished by the change of attitude towards joint residence orders as shown in the case of *A v A (Children: Shared residence order)* (1994). Even though such orders will still only be granted in unusual circumstances and when the court can see definite benefit for the child it could assist a party to provide continuity of care for part of the time when he may be unable to do during the whole period.

## The likely effect on the child of any change in his or her circumstances

The court may also consider that on balance it is usually best to maintain the status quo as any unnecessary disruption could be against the welfare of the child and stability is an important factor during his early years.

The case of *J v C* (1970) illustrates the importance the court attributes to maintaining the status quo. In this case the court awarded custody of the child to his foster parents who lived in England rather than to his natural parents who lived in Spain as the boy was deemed to be better off staying in this country and had spent all but 18 months of his life here.

What will be regarded as the status quo will depend on the length of time that the prevailing circumstances have existed. A short period will not be seen as sufficient to establish a new status quo as in the case of *Allington v Allington* (1985) where a period of 10 weeks was said to be too short to set a new status quo.

However, in *Re H (A Minor: Custody)* (1990) a child who had spent one and a half years in this country after being brought here by his father to live with his aunt and uncle. This was seen as the status quo and should be maintained even though the mother who still lived in India was a loving and caring person it was considered that the boy's interests would be best served by remaining in this country.

It must be remembered that each case will ultimately depend on its own circumstances and if the welfare of the child dictates a certain course of action then the court will do what it sees as necessary. In *Re G (Minors)* (1992) the children were removed from the mother who had had custody for three years and they were placed with their father. The mother had admitted using drugs in the presence of the children.

## The child's age sex background and any characteristics of the child which the court considers relevant

This item covers a general area for consideration by the courts and more than any other will depend on the particular circumstances involved. Factors that could be considered will be whether girls should live with their mothers or boys should live with their fathers. Also factors such as ethnic or religious background should be examined along with any significant cultural aspects that the court considers relevant. Considerations that arise in previous sections can also be covered by this general heading.

## Any harm which the child has suffered or is at risk of suffering

This item is of great significance in both private and public law matters. The court has a basic duty to prevent harm and one way in which this can be done is to look at who is to provide the care and how it is to be provided. As these orders are frequently sought on the breakdown of marriage it is often the case that a parent has a new partner and if this parent is seeking the order then the attributes of the new partner are of importance if he is to form part of a new household. In *Scott v Scott* (1986) the mother's new partner had a criminal record which included offences of indecency against children.

Although the factor of religion now receives less attention than it did in the past it is still an area that can cause some concern. The court will look at the nature of any religious sect that may be involved in the child's life and will consider whether or not there is any potential danger or harm that could arise with respect to the child.

The type of matter that is often considered in this area is that of the difficulty that could occur if the child of a Jehovah's witness parent required a blood transfusion during medical treatment. This would not necessarily preclude such a parent from being granted an order since under the Children Act both parents retain parental responsibility even after divorce and in matters of medical treatment either party can consent to treatment. This could preclude any problem for the medical staff as each party can act independently for the welfare of the child as long as they do not breach a court order. The court also has available prohibited steps orders or specific steps orders and can make appropriate use of these orders to deal with such matters without necessarily having to grant residence to the non-religious partner.

The sexual preferences of a parent may also need consideration and a number of cases concerning lesbian mothers have been reported and an overview of recent decisions would seem to indicate that the courts are taking a more enlightened and liberal view.

In earlier cases the court held fears that the child could suffer emotionally from such relationships and have their sexuality affected and could suffer from the intolerance of other children at school and from other members of the community who became aware of the home situation.

The correct approach is that now such parents are not necessarily precluded from having the children but the situation still has to be looked at and a proper balance sought.

In *C v C (A Minor) (Custody Appeal)* (1991) it was stated that the ideal situation was that the child should be brought up in the family set-up nearest to the accepted norm, ie the usual heterosexual family. If this was not possible then the circumstances of the case needed to be considered and the court should decide the matter on the welfare of the child.

In this case the judge had considered the fact that the mother was a lesbian was of no relevance and granted her custody. On appeal it was stated that the factor was relevant and should be considered and the case was remitted for rehearing. On consideration of the facts the child remained with the mother and her female partner.

*B v B (Minors) (Custody Care and Control)* (1991) is another example of when the court has granted the custody of the child to a lesbian mother after a full consideration of the facts. Here the mother's case was helped by a psychiatrist's report which said that the fears that were commonly held in such situations were greatly exaggerated and did not apply in the present case. The mother was seen as being able to provide the highest standard of care and was granted custody.

### The capability of each parent of meeting the child's needs

The factors that can be considered here are the basic common sense factors which should be obvious when looking at the needs of a child. The parent should show his capability of providing love and care, accommodation and adequate resources to allow the child to develop to his full potential. The factors mentioned in the other areas dealt with above should also be looked at here.

## The range of powers available to the court under the Children Act 1989

As this area falls within the definition of 'family proceedings' s 8 orders are available to the court whether there has been an application or at its own motion. It can also make orders under s 16 family assistance orders with the consent of the parties named in the orders, orders appointing guardians and under s 37 can direct the local authority to investigate a child's circumstances with the view that it may be appropriate for the local authority to apply for a care order or supervision order.

However s 1(5) – the 'no order principle' – must always be borne in mind when considering whether or not to make any order. It is fundamental to the philosophy of the Act and it's importance cannot be overemphasised.

If there has been conflict in the area but the parties reach agreement prior to the proceedings then usually the court will allow the arrangements to stand as to do otherwise could be seen as interference by the court with one party being favoured over the other and this could cause further hostility and bitterness with adverse effects resulting for the child. However, the court must always base its judgment on the welfare of the child.

## Financial provision and property adjustment for children

Section 15 and Schedule 1 of the Children Act 1989 set out the provisions for financial relief for children. An application for financial relief comes within the definition of 'family proceedings' and a court hearing such an application may also make s 8 orders. The orders the court can make are orders for periodical payments, lump sums, settlements and transfers of property. However, if the application is made in the family proceedings court then only the monetary orders are available, not the property orders.

The court can make such orders against parents and step-parents in relation to whom the child concerned is a child of the family.

The definition of 'child of the family' is contained in s 105(1):

- a child of both those parties;
- any other child, not being a child who is placed with those parties as foster parents by a local authority or voluntary organisation who has been treated by both those parties as a child of their family.

When deciding whether or not to exercise its power against a person who is not the mother or father of the child the court must have regard to:

- whether that person had assumed responsibility for the maintenance of the child and if so the extent to which, and basis on which, he assumed that responsibility and the length of the period during which he met that responsibility;
- whether he did so knowing that the child was not his child;
- the liability of any other person to maintain the child.

Applications for such orders can be made by either parent, married or unmarried, step-parents, guardians and people with residence orders in their favour with respect to the child.

Also an application can be made by a child of 18 years or over who either is, will be or would be (if the order were made) receiving educational instruction or vocational training or where special circumstances exist. However, such an order cannot be made if the applicant's parents are living together in the same household and/or an order for periodical payments was in force in favour of the applicant immediately before he reached the age of 16. Also the court is restricted to making periodical payments and/or lump sums in such cases and only against natural and adoptive parents.

### The matters the court will consider

These are contained in Schedule 1 para 4 and are:

- the income, earning capacity, property and other financial resources the parents have;
- the financial needs, obligations and responsibilities the parents have;
- the financial needs of the child;
- the income, earning capacity property and other financial resources of the child;
- any physical or mental disability of the child;
- the manner in which the child was being or was expected to be educated or trained.

However, it must be noted that in these matters the child's welfare is not paramount when deciding matters of financial provision and the court must apply the statutory guidelines as was stated in *K v K (Minors: Property Transfer)* (1992).

# Guardianship

The position is now much more restricted than prior to the implementation of the Children Act and the only methods of making an appointment are contained in s 5 of the Act.

Section 5(1) gives the court the power to appoint an individual who applies to be a guardian with respect to a child if:

- the child has no parent with parental responsibility for him; or
- a residence order has been made with respect to the child in favour of a parent or guardian who has died while the order was in force.

Section 5(2) allows the court to make an appointment in the above circumstances even if no application is made if it is considered necessary.

Section 5(1)(a) covers the situation where both parents are dead and no guardian has been appointed. It also applies where an unmarried mother has died as the unmarried father will not have parental responsibility unless arrangements have been made for him to acquire it by way of an agreement with the mother or by way of a court order.

The father could also gain guardianship if he has been appointed by the mother prior to her death or he could apply and be appointed as a guardian by the court.

Section 5(1)(b) allows an appointment where a residence order was made in favour of a parent or a guardian who has since died. This equates with the parent's power to make a private appointment.

This power covers situations such as where a divorced parent who had a residence order in his favour has died and it is considered that the surviving parent who has no residence order in her favour may not be suitable to be allowed to automatically be entitled to assume care of the child because she has parental responsibility which, in other circumstances, would allow her to take action as long as it would not be incompatible with a court order.

Where the parent with the residence order may have anticipated this problem he could make an appointment for the intended guardian to share parental responsibility with the other partner but if he has failed to do so then the court can use it's power to appoint a guardian. If the precaution has been taken, however, and a problem arises between the guardian and the surviving parent then the court can use its powers, usually s 8 orders to determine the matter.

Persons with parental responsibility have power under s 5(3) and (4) to make private appointments of guardians. Remember that unmarried fathers need to acquire parental responsibility to be able to appoint a guardian.

Section 5(3) allows a parent with parental responsibility for his child to appoint another individual to be the child's guardian in the event of his death.

Section 5(4) allows a guardian of a child to appoint another individual to take his place as the child's guardian in the event of his death.

Although the sections mention the word 'individual' it is thought that more than one person can be appointed.

The appointment can be made by will but need not be. It will be effective if the appointment is made in writing, dated and signed at the direction of the person making the appointment in his presence and in the presence of two witnesses.

It must be borne in mind that the appointment will only take effect on the death of the surviving parent with parental responsibility and the inherent jurisdiction of the court can no longer be used to appoint a guardian except where provision is made by rules of court.

Guardians will gain parental responsibility for the child on their appointment and will be able to consent to the child's adoption.

## The revocation and disclaimer of an appointment

Section 6 says that a later appointment by a parent or guardian will be taken to revoke the earlier appointment unless it is clear (either by express provision or necessary implication) that the purpose of the later appointment is to make an additional appointment.

It also allows the parent to revoke the appointment by another written document which meets the requirements needed for an appointment or by destroying the original document. If the appointment is made by will then this must be revoked.

If a person has been appointed as a child's guardian but wishes to disclaim his appointment then he can do so by an instrument in writing signed by him and it must be made within a reasonable time of his first knowing that the appointment has taken effect. The obvious way to avoid difficulties would be to consult with the person to be appointed prior to making the arrangements thus making a disclaimer unnecessary.

The court has the power to bring an appointment of a guardian to an end on the application of any person with parental responsibility, on the application of the child concerned with leave of the court and in any family proceedings if the court considers it should be brought to an end even though no application has been made.

The court when dealing with matters of guardianship should apply the principles contained in s 1(1)(2) and (5) and although it need not apply the checklist in s 1(3), it will normally do so.

# Revision Notes

## Parents and Children

### Duties and responsibilities

- Parental responsibility s 3(1) CA 1989.
- Shared by married parents.
- Acquired by unmarried fathers by use of s 4 CA 1989.
- Ability to act independently.

### Children Act 1989

#### New philosophy
- Non-intervention unless really necessary.
- Consistency and flexibility of orders at all levels.

#### Founding principles
- Section 1(1) welfare is paramount.
- Section 1(2) no delay.
- *C v Solihull MBC* (1993).
- Section 1(3) checklist.
- Section 1(5) 'no order'.
- *B v B (Grandparents: Residence Order)* 1992.

#### New orders

*Residence order*
- *A v A (Children:Shared Residence Order)* (1994).
- Section 13 restrictions – surname and removal from jurisdiction.
- *W v A (Child.Surname)* (1981).

*Contact order*
- Right of the child not of the parent.
- *M v M* (1973).
- *Re J(A Minor)(Contact)* (1994).
- *Nottingham CC v P* (1993).

*Prohibited steps order*

*Specific issue order*
- Restriction on their use – s 91(5).

- Need to show the meeting of aspect of parental responsibility.
- Who can apply? Section 10.
- Section 10(4): The following persons are entitled to apply to the court for any s 8 order with respect to a child:
  (a)     any parent or guardian of the child;
  (b)     any person in whose favour a residence order is in force with respect to the child.
- Section 10(5): The following persons are entitled to apply for a residence or contact order with respect to the child
  (a)     any party to a marriage (whether or not subsisting) in relation to whom the child is a child of the family;
  (b)     any person with whom the child has lived for a period of at least three years;
  (c)     any person who –
  (i)     in any case where a residence order is in force with respect to the child has the consent of each of the persons in whose favour the order was made
  (ii)    in any case where the child is in the care of the local authority has the consent of that authority
  (iii)   in any other case has the consent of each of those (if any) who have parental responsibility for the child.
- Section 10(9) leave requirements:
  (a)     The child may also apply but will require leave.
  (b)     When considering leave the welfare principle does not apply.
  (c)     *Re A & W (Minors:Residence Order)(Leave to Apply)* (1992).
- Section 16 family assistance order.
  (a)     The need for consent from all parties other than the child.
  (b)     No applications can be made for this order,the court will make it on its own motion. Lasts for 6 months maximum.

## Private law

### Family breakdown

*Effects of Section 25 and Section 41 MCA 1973*
Checklist contents.
Section 1(3):
(a)   the ascertainable wishes and feelings of the child concerned (considered in the light of his age and understanding;
(b)   his physical emotional and educational needs;
(c)   the likely effect on him of any change in his circumstances;

(d) his age sex background and any other characteristics of his which the court considers relevant;

(e) any harm which he has suffered or is at risk of suffering;

(f) how capable each of his parents and any other person in relation to whom the court considers the question to be relevant is of meeting his needs;

(g) the range of powers available to the court under this Act in the proceedings in question.

### Financial provisions for children

*Section 15 Schedule 1*
Orders available for children.
- Periodical payments, lump sums.
- Property adjustment orders.
- Applicants, parents, step-parents, person with residence orders in force with respect to the child.
- Children within limits.

### Considerations
Schedule 1 para 4.

### Guardianship

*Section 5 CA 1989*
Appointments.
- Can be made by the parents or the court but will only become effective in the event of death.
- Methods of appointment.
- Section 6 Revocation/disclaimer.
- Methods of revocation.

# 7 Children II

## Public law

When looking at the relationship between children and local authorities the examinable areas in family law are those of care and supervision orders and child protection orders.

### Care and supervision orders

Since the Children Act 1989 came into effect there is now only one way that a child can be placed into the care of a local authority or be made subject to a supervision order and that is by the applicant being able to satisfy the requirements of Section 31(2) of the Act and showing that the welfare of the child demands that the order be made. Wardship can no longer be used to make a child the subject of these orders.

Most care proceedings will commence in the family proceedings court but matters may be transferred to a county court or the High Court if it is considered appropriate since all these courts have jurisdiction to deal with care matters as they fall within the definition of 'family proceedings'.

## Who can apply for a care or supervision order?

Under s 31(1) applications for such orders can only be made by:

- a local authority; or
- an authorised person.

At the present time the only 'authorised person' is the NSPCC although the Secretary of State has the power to name others at some future date.

If the court is dealing with matters that are considered to be 'family proceedings' and it considers that a local authority should investigate the circumstances of the case it has the power to direct that the authority should do so (s 37(1)).

However, if the authority carries out the investigation but decides that an application for a care order is not, in its opinion, necessary, then the court cannot require the authority to make an application and this could mean that situations may arise when children may be left without measures being available to safeguard their welfare as occurred in the case of *Nottinghamshire County Council v P* (1993).

A care order or supervision order can only be made with respect to a child who is under 17 years of age (or 16 if the child is married).

## The threshold criteria

When the local authority has decided that an application is to be made then it must be able to fulfil the requirements of s 31(2) which have become known as the 'threshold criteria'.

Section 31(2) states:

The court may only make a care order or a supervision order if it is satisfied:

(a)    that the child concerned is suffering, or is likely to suffer, significant harm; and

(b)    that the harm, or likelihood of harm, is attributable to –

    (i)    the care given to the child, or likely to be given him if the order were not made, not being what it would be reasonable to expect a parent to give him; or

    (ii)   the child's being beyond parental control.

Both parts of the section must be satisfied. The harm element must be shown to be present but also that the harm is being caused by either the care the child is receiving or that he is beyond control.

A vital element to remember is that even when the authority has been able to satisfy the 'threshold criteria' the court will be required to consider the contents of s 1 of the Act.

The welfare principle, delay principle and the 'no order' principle must be borne in mind before the final decision is made. They form the basis of the court's decision in all 'family proceedings'.

Section 31(9) contains the definitions of the terms used in the 'threshold criteria'.

'Harm':    ill-treatment or the impairment of health and development.

'Development': physical, intellectual, emotional, social or behavioural development.

'Health':    physical or mental health.

'Ill-treatment': includes sexual abuse and other forms of ill-treatment which are not physical.

Difficulty could arise when trying to apply the word 'significant'. It is not defined in the Act and a great deal will depend on the circumstances of the case. Minor failings should not require intervention but if they occur frequently or have a cumulative effect on the child then they could be regarded as 'significant'.

When looking at the effect of any failings on the child s 31(10) states that the child in question must be judged against what can be expected of a similar child having taken into account the characteristics of that child ie take a subjective view of the child in question and apply an objective test when comparing him with a similar child.

'Care' is not defined in the Act but is generally accepted as including the normal physical and emotional care that a reasonable parent would give a child.

The House of Lords decision in *Re M (A Minor) (Care Order: Threshold Conditions)* (1994) has settled that the time when judgment has to be made about significant harm being suffered is when the local authority commences proceedings for the protection of the child. This means the time the local authority takes any temporary measure that may lead to a care order application being made in the future.

The question of future harm which the child is 'likely to suffer' should not be judged as just 'on the balance of probabilities'. The court should look at all the evidence and decide whether or not he will suffer harm in the future if no order is made. It has been held that the words should not be construed restrictively and a care order should be granted if indicated by the evidence (*Re A (A Minor) (Care Proceedings)* (1993)).

When looking at the second part of the criteria, the harm being considered must arise from the care being given by the child's parent not being what would be expected from a reasonable parent ie an objective test.

However, when looking at the element of being 'beyond parental control' it need not be the parent's fault. It may be that the parent has tried to discipline the child but has failed, the child would then be beyond control and could be the subject of an application. The parent could ask the local authority to make such an application but it will be up to the authority to decide whether or not to do so.

The 'threshold criteria' are the minimum standards that must be reached to obtain a care order or a supervision order. The court will retain the discretion whether or not to make the order after considering s 1 of the Act. It could arise that the court will judge that it would be best for the child that a s 8 order be made and if a residence order is made in such proceedings it must also make an interim supervision order unless the child's welfare is safeguarded without such an order (s 38(3)).

## The effects of a care order

While a care order is in force with respect to the child the local authority will have parental responsibility for him (s 33). This does not mean that the parents have lost their parental responsibility (s 2(5)) but it will mean that they share it with the authority and the authority can determine the extent to which the parents or guardians can meet their parental responsibility towards the child (s 33(3)(b)).

However, the authority should not seek to limit the parents exercise of their parental responsibility unless it is necessary to do so in order to safeguard or promote the welfare of the child (s 33(4)).

The existence of the care order will discharge all existing s 8 orders, any supervision order and will terminate wardship (s 91).

There are further restrictions placed on the local authority.

The authority may not:

- change the child's religion;
- change the child's name;
- agree or refuse to agree to the child's adoption;
- consent or refuse to the making of a freeing order;
- change the child's surname or remove him from the UK without the written consent of every person with  parental responsibility for the child or the leave of the court.

It is important to remember that the court will not interfere with the way the local authority will implement a care order. Since it is seen that Parliament intended that local authorities should be trusted to do as they see fit when dealing with children in their care and the court, having had the opportunity to study the authority's plan when deciding to make the order, should allow the authority to manage the situation and should not attach conditions to a care order (*Re T (A Minor) (Care Order: Conditions)* (1994)).

## Parental contact with a child in care

Contact between the child and his parents, guardian, any person with a residence order in force with respect to the child or any person who has care of the child under the inherent jurisdiction of the court immediately prior to the granting of the care order is considered to be of importance when looking at the matter of the child's welfare.

Section 34 of the Act states that there is a statutory presumption that the authority must allow the child to have reasonable contact with these groups of people after the granting of the order and the authority is expected to present its proposals for contact in its plans put before the court.

However, if the authority deems it necessary to terminate contact between the child and the parent then it must apply to the court to do so under s 34(4). The court will base its decision on the principles in s 1 of the Act and can refuse contact for as long as the child's welfare demands (*West Glamorgan County Council v P* (No 1) (1992)).

There is also provision for the authority to refuse contact, as a matter of urgency, between the child and his parent for up to a period of seven days where this is necessary for the child's welfare (s 34(6)). If the authority deems this necessary then it must give written notice of that decision to the child concerned (if the child is of sufficient understanding) and to the people with whom he will be presumed to have contact.

## The effects of a supervision order

When an application has been made under s 31(1) the court has the power to grant either a care order or a supervision order if the authority has fulfilled the 'threshold criteria'.

A supervision order does not give the local authority parental responsibility for the child. However, it does impose a duty on the local authority or a probation officer to advise assist and befriend the child.

The supervisor must take such steps as are as necessary to give effect to the order and must also consider whilst the order is in force whether or not to vary or discharge the order. This is to prevent a situation arising where matters are just allowed to drift with nothing being done.

The supervisor has been given new powers to give directions to the child and to seek the help of any 'responsible person' ie any person who has parental responsibility for the child and any other person with whom the child is living, by imposing obligations on such persons although this can only be done with their consent.

These obligations can require the responsible person to take all reasonable steps to ensure that the child complies with directions given by the supervisor, to take all reasonable steps to ensure that the child complies with any requirement concerning psychiatric or medical examination or treatment and to comply with any directions to attend at a specified place to take part in specified activities.

The aim of these measures is to try and ensure that the supervisor gets as much assistance as he can from such people in an attempt to get the best results from the supervision order.

The directions the supervisor can give to the child can include that the child should live in a certain place, attend certain places and partake in certain activities. A child can also be directed to have a medical or psychiatric examination but certain conditions must be satisfied.

The child must consent if he has sufficient understanding and satisfactory arrangements have been or can be made for the examination.

A supervision order will cease to have effect after one year but the supervisor can apply for the order to be extended for up to three years.

### Interim care and supervision orders

In certain circumstances the court will be unable to reach a conclusion as to how to finally deal with a case and may need to make an interim order until further enquiries have been made and reports submitted for its consideration.

When such a situation arises the 'delay principle' in s 1(2) must be borne in mind ie delay is detrimental to the child's welfare. This is why the duration of interim orders are limited and the orders are only available if proceedings are adjourned or the court gives a direction under s 37 of the Act requiring the local authority to investigate the child's circumstances. The court must have reasonable grounds to believe that the threshold criteria can be satisfied.

An interim supervision order must be made if, in care proceedings, the court makes a residence order with respect to the child unless it is satisfied that the child's welfare will be safeguarded without it.

Interim orders will last for up to a maximum of eight weeks but there is no limit to the number that can be made.

## Discharge of a care order

A care order can be discharged on an application by a person with parental responsibility for the child, the child himself or the local authority (s 39).

The court will decide the matter on the principles contained in s 1 of the Act.

The persons with parental responsibility for the child in these circumstances are the married parents, the unmarried mother, the unmarried father with parental responsibility and the child's guardian.

If other persons wish to seek an end to the order the only way they have of achieving this is to apply for a residence order which if granted will bring an end to the care order (s 91(1)). However, to do this they would require the leave of the court unless such application is made by the unmarried father who does not have parental responsibility.

A residence order, if granted, will vest parental responsibility in the applicant and if he is the unmarried father then the court will also be required to make an order giving him parental responsibility (s 12(1)).

In practice it will usually be the local authority that will seek the discharge of the care order as at the regular case conferences that are held concerning children in care it is required to consider whether or not to apply for a discharge of the care order and often conclude that it would be in the best interests of the child to do so. However, the authority could decide to apply to discharge the care order and find that the court could replace it with a supervision order which it could do without the need to satisfy the requirements of s 31(2).

If an application to discharge a care order or to replace a care order with a supervision order is refused then no further application can be made within six months except with the leave of the court (s 91(5)).

## Variation of supervision orders

A supervision order can be varied or discharged by any person who has parental responsibility for the child, the child himself or the supervisor. A person with whom the child lives who is not in these groups of applicants can also seek a variation of the supervision order to the extent of any requirement that affects him.

## Appointment of a guardian *ad litem*

Section 41(1) of the Act states that in care and supervision proceedings a guardian *ad litem* must be appointed to represent the child unless a guardian is not needed to safeguard the child's interests.

The guardian who is usually an independent social worker ie is not employed by the local authority involved in the proceedings has the general duty to safeguard the child's interests and will attempt to do so by ascertaining the child's understanding of the situation, ascertaining his wishes and investigating the circumstances of the case. The guardian has the power to gain access to the local authority records and can use the information in evidence during the case (Section 42).

When the guardian has completed his task he will submit a written report to the court with his views as what would be best for the child. The court will consider any matter raised in the report in so far as it is relevant to the matters being considered by the court regardless of any act or rule of law which would otherwise make the evidence inadmissible (s 41(11)). The court will usually give considerable weight to this report.

A solicitor may also be appointed by the guardian unless one has already been appointed by the court. He will give the solicitor instructions on the child's behalf unless the child has sufficient understanding to do so himself.

## Emergency protection of children

Part V of the Children Act contains the measures intended to provide emergency protection for children. This part of the Act does not fall within the definition of 'family proceedings' and so the court will be unable to make s 8 orders when dealing with these applications.

When dealing with matters under Part V the court's decisions will be based on the welfare of the child being the paramount consideration, the delay principle and the 'no order' principle. It will not consider the matters contained in the checklist as it is dealing with a short-term remedy for an emergency situation.

## Child assessment orders

Under s 43(1) an application for a child assessment order can only be made by a local authority or the NSPCC. The court can make the order if it is satisfied that:

- the applicant has reasonable cause to suspect that the child is suffering or is likely to suffer significant harm;
- an assessment of the state of the child's health or development or of the way in which he has been treated is required to enable the applicant to determine whether or not the child is suffering or is likely to suffer significant harm; and
- it is unlikely that such an assessment will be made or be satisfactory in the absence of an order under this section.

The applicant must take reasonable steps to give notice to the child's parents or carers or persons with parental responsibility or a contact order with respect to the child and the child.

The court will base its decision on the child's welfare and the order will require the parents or carers to produce the child for assessment or allow the child to be visited to allow an assessment to be carried out. This means that the child can remain with the family whilst any assessment is carried out. If the child has to go elsewhere for assessment eg a hospital and has to stay away from home for a few days then the court can give directions as to contact and may specify the length of time he can be kept there.

The court should also specify in the order the kind of assessment which is required, the date on which it is to begin and how long it will last, which must be no longer than seven days from that date.

It should also specify how to make the assessment but a child of sufficient understanding can refuse to undergo any form of assessment contained in the order (s 43(8)).

If the parents refuse to comply with the assessment order there appears to be no direct form of enforcement. However, the local authority could inform them that if they continue to fail to comply with the order it could lead to the authority making an application for an emergency protection order.

An important point to bear in mind when considering whether or not to grant an assessment order is that if the court thinks that the grounds exist for the granting of an emergency protection order then the court may treat the application as an application for an emergency protection order and grant the order if the grounds are shown to exist (s 43(4)).

## Emergency protection orders

The classes of persons allowed to apply for an emergency protection order and the grounds on which it will be granted are contained in s 44 of the Act.

Section 44(1)(a) states that any person may apply for such an order and the court will grant the order if it satisfied that there is reasonable cause to believe that the child is likely to suffer significant harm if either:

- he is not removed to accommodation provided by or on behalf of the applicant; or
- he does not remain in the place where he is then being accommodated.

Although this section allows 'any person' to apply in practice it will usually be a local authority making the application.

The local authority may also apply under s 44(1)(b) when the court must be satisfied that:

- enquiries are being made with respect to the child under s 47(1)(b) (ie where the authority has the duty to investigate whether a child is suffering or is likely to suffer significant harm); and
- those enquiries are being frustrated by access to the child being unreasonably refused to a person authorised to seek access and that the applicant has reasonable cause to believe that access to the child is a matter of urgency.

Applications made by the NSPCC can also be made on similar grounds contained in s 44(1)(c).

Applications are usually made to the family proceedings court of the magistrates' court and in an extreme situation can be made *ex parte* to a single justice although ideally the hearing should be inter partes. If the application is made *ex parte* then the order must be served on the parents within 48 hours.

The order can be granted for up to eight days but on a subsequent application the court can grant one extension for up to seven days making a total of 15 days in all. This measure is an attempt to ensure that the applicant will take the necessary action with the minimum delay.

## The effects of an emergency protection order

Section 44(4) allows the court to direct any person who is in a position to do so to produce the child to the applicant and authorises the removal to, or retention in, accommodation provided by the applicant, or prevents the removal of the child from some other place where the child was being accommodated immediately prior to the order.

It is an offence to prevent the removal of the child or to obstruct a person exercising the power to remove the child.

The court may give directions when the emergency protection order is made. They will usually deal with an assessment of the child by way of medical or psychiatric examination but the child, if of sufficient understanding, may refuse to comply with the examination or assessment. The court can, if the circumstances require it, also direct that no such examination should be carried out.

The other usual direction attached to these orders concerns contact between the child and his parents, those with parental responsibility for the child, those with whom the child was living immediately prior to the order and any person acting on behalf of those people. The authority should allow the child to have reasonable contact with these groups.

The order vests limited parental responsibility for the child in the applicant for the duration of the order. However, s 44(5) limits the applicant's use of parental responsibility to what is required to safeguard or promote the welfare of the child.

The authority should only remove the child from his home for as long as is necessary for the child's welfare and should return him home as soon as it is safe to do so. However, if the applicant considers that he needs to remove the child again during the existence of the order then he has the power to do so.

No appeal can be made against the granting of an emergency protection order but an application to discharge the order can be made but only after 72 hours have elapsed after the granting of the order. Such applications can be made by the child, his parents, someone with parental responsibility for the child or any person with whom the child was living immediately prior to the order. However, the application cannot be made if the person received notice of the hearing and was present at the hearing or if the order has been extended.

## Wardship and the inherent jurisdiction

The wardship jurisdiction of the court is used to protect the interests of children and parental responsibility for the child rests with the court. If wardship is granted then the child will often stay with the party that made the application but that party will not be able to take any important step in the child's life without the consent of the court which can also give directions to safeguard the welfare of the child (*Re S* (1967).

Wardship proceedings fall within the definition of 'family proceedings' for the purposes of the Children Act 1989 as they are part of the inherent jurisdiction of the High Court. This allows the court to make the orders that are contained within the Act except where there are restrictions such as when the child is the care of the local authority and subject to a care order.

When the court considers whether to make any order contained within the Children Act the welfare of the child is the paramount consideration when considering matters concerned with the child's upbringing or the administration of the child's property.

The inherent jurisdiction of the High Court is the use of the power of the Crown as *parens patriae*. This stems from the duty of the Crown to protect its subjects. The inherent jurisdiction is theoretically without limit but in practice there are limits that apply. Where the inherent jurisdiction applies to children it gives the court the ability to exceed the powers and overrule the decisions of parents and 'Gillick competent' children (*Re W (A Minor) (Consent to Medical Treatment)* (1993)).

The inherent jurisdiction exists independently of wardship and can be used to protect the interests of a child that has not been made a ward. It is generally used to settle a specific issue, very often a medical matter, and will be used when there are no statutory provisions available to settle the issue.

## Wardship and the Children Act 1989

The Children Act has, as we have seen, introduced a flexible range of orders which are available to the court when dealing with 'family proceedings'. This has made the use of wardship much less likely than previously and generally it will only be necessary in cases where the orders are unavailable.

### Private law matters

The Children Act has not placed any restriction on the use of wardship in private law matters. However, the wide range of powers in s 8 of the Act makes it more likely that the parties will use these orders rather than use wardship.

There will be times when there could be an advantage to using wardship. This could be if there is a leave requirement under the

Children Act then the use of wardship will avoid this. Also if the element of continuing judicial control is thought to be necessary then again wardship will be the better route to take (*Re G-U (A Minor) (Wardship)* (1984).

## Public law matters

Unlike private law matters the area of public law has been severely restricted by the Children Act. Section 100(2) ensures that local authorities are no longer allowed to use wardship or the inherent jurisdiction to take children into care or make them subject to a supervision order. They must now use the statutory procedures contained in the Children Act and they must satisfy the 'threshold' criteria in s 31(2). This is yet another example of the philosophy contained in the Act ie that of non-intervention by the state.

Another restriction imposed by s 100(2) is that a child who is the subject of a care order cannot be made a ward of court. This was permitted prior to the Act if the local authority agreed to it.

Under the current situation if a ward is committed to the care of a local authority then the warship will cease to have effect (s 91(4)).

The question of parental responsibility also arises when dealing with children and s 100(2)(d) prohibits the use of the inherent jurisdiction by a local authority to gain any element of parental responsibility when deciding any question regarding the upbringing of a child. The court cannot confer the local authority with any degree of parental responsibility that it does not already have.

However, there are situations when local authorities are still able to use the inherent jurisdiction albeit with the leave of the court (s 100(3)).

To grant leave the court must be satisfied that:

- the result that the local authority wish to achieve could not be achieved by the making of any other type of order which the local authority might be entitled to apply for under the statutory code; and
- there is reasonable cause to believe that if the court's inherent jurisdiction is not exercised with respect to the child he is likely to suffer significant harm.

This limits the local authority to using its statutory powers unless there is a need for a supplementary power to deal with a particular problem. The usual types of cases that are dealt with in this area concern specific issues such as medical problems that occur when a child needs emergency treatment as in the case of *Re E (A Minor: Medical Treatment)* (1993) when a child of Jehovah Witnesses required a blood transfusion or where an abortion is being sought as in the cases of *Re D (A Minor) (Wardship: Sterilisation)* (1976) and *Re B (A Minor) (Wardship: Sterilisation)* (1987).

When dealing with such applications the court must be satisfied that the request is being made in the best interests of the child and not in the interests of the local authority.

The usual applicants for wardship are either local authorities or parents but an application can be made by any person who must state their relationship with the child and must also be able to show a sufficient interest in the matter. The child himself may also apply to be made a ward with leave of the court by way of his next friend or also without his next friend provided that he has sufficient understanding.

Wardship proceedings are commenced in the Family Division of the High Court by originating summons and the minor automatically becomes a ward as soon as the originating summons is issued (s 41(2) Supreme Court Act 1981).

The court will look closely at the application to see if there is an abuse of process as was present in the case of *Re Dunhill* (1973) when a night-club owner tried to make one of his models a ward. The application was struck out as being vexatious and an abuse of process.

The type of situation that occurs in wardship is often concerned with medical matters and with decisions as to whether or not medical treatment is to be performed on the child.

It would be useful to compare the cases of *Re Baby J* (1990) and *Re B (A Minor) (Wardship: Medical Treatment)* (1981).

In *Re Baby J* the child was born with a severe handicap and suffered from a life-threatening condition. The child was made a ward and the High Court had to consider the matter of medical treatment which in effect meant was the child to live or die.

The decision was to be dealt with on the basis that the child's welfare was the paramount consideration.

It was held that the treatment would produce no benefit for the child but would lead to increased suffering and the court would be justified in refusing to consent to medical treatment.

In *Re B* the child's parents refused consent to medical treatment and the local authority made the child a ward to obtain the court's consent to an operation that would save the child's life. The court held that the child's welfare would be best served by allowing the treatment and gave its consent.

There is a strong presumption that life should be preserved but it was a rebuttable presumption. The welfare of the child was of paramount importance and this would be the decisive factor.

Where other difficult questions arise as to medical treatment such as abortion and sterilisation then there will often be Practice Directions in existence that will need to be observed.

### Publicity

In wardship proceedings the court has the power to make an injunction prohibiting the publication of information that is considered harmful to the child. Any order made is binding on every person who is potentially subject to the order even though they have not been joined as a party to the proceedings.

Although the publication of information relating to proceeding before any court sitting in private is not in itself a contempt. However, there are exceptions to this situation and these include:

- proceedings which relate to the exercise of the inherent jurisdiction of the High Court in relation to minors;
- proceedings under the Children Act 1989.
- any other proceedings which relate wholly or mainly to the maintenance or upbringing of a minor.

When deciding such matters the court will NOT regard the welfare of the child as paramount but it will regard the child's welfare as the most important consideration. The balance the court will seek to achieve when reaching its decision will be between that of the welfare of the child and that of the public interest (*Re H (Minors) (Public Interest: Protection of Identity)* (1993)).

## Adoption

The legislation covering the matter of adoption is contained in the Adoption Act 1976.

An adoption order brings a legal adoption into being and ends a natural parent's parental responsibility and vests it in the adoptive parents. It also ends any parental responsibility that any other person may have had for the child and brings to an end any order made under the Children Act 1989. However, such proceedings fall within the definition of 'family proceedings' and as such the court will be able to make use of s 8 orders in such proceedings should they consider them necessary.

Adoption agencies are responsible for arranging adoptions unless the prospective adopter is a relative or a person acting under a High Court order. Adoption agencies are run by local authorities or approved voluntary adoption societies and in practice most local authorities will run the service within its area.

## The welfare of the child

Section 6 of the Adoption Act 1976 states that:

In reaching any decision in relation to the adoption of a child a court or adoption agency must have regard to all the circumstances, first consideration being given to the need to safeguard and promote the welfare of the child throughout his childhood; and shall so far as practicable ascertain the wishes and feelings of the child regarding the decision and give due consideration to them, having regard to his age and understanding.

Thus it must be noted that the child's welfare is not paramount but is the first consideration.

## Freeing for adoption

Section 18(1) of the Adoption Act allows an adoption agency to apply to the court for a 'freeing order' which declares that the child is free for adoption. This must be made with the consent of the parents or guardian unless the agency is applying to dispense with that consent as it is able to do under s 18 (1)(b).

This application can only be made by a local authority as 'freeing orders' only apply to children who are in care.

The court can only make a 'freeing order' if it is satisfied that each parent or guardian with parental responsibility has consented freely and with understanding of what is involved in making an adoption order or that such consent can be dispensed with on the grounds contained in s 16(2).

The consent of the unmarried father is not required but the court must be satisfied that he does not intend to apply for a parental responsibility order or for a residence order or that if he did make such an application it would be likely to be refused.

If a 'freeing order' is granted it will vest parental responsibility in the adoption agency and the parents or guardian cannot veto the adoption. The advantage for the adoption agency is that it can plan for the future of the child without the fear of interference in its plans. It also has the same effect as an adoption order in that it will bring to an end any order under the Children Act.

If after 12 months after the 'freeing order' being granted an adoption order has not been made and the child does not have his home with the person with whom he was placed for adoption a parent or guardian can apply for the 'freeing order' to be revoked on the ground that he wishes to resume parental responsibility for the child. Such revocation will remove the agency's parental responsibility and gives it back to the parent. It will also revive any parental responsibility agreement and guardianship appointment but will not revive any other Children Act order. It will not affect the parental responsibility held by the local authority prior to the 'freeing order' ie the care order.

## Adoption order

When the court makes an adoption order it extinguishes the parental responsibility of the natural parents and gives it to the adoptive parents (s 12(1)).

When it decides whether or not to make an adoption order the court must apply the provisions of s 6 but may not make an order unless it is satisfied that sufficient opportunities to see the child together with one or both the applicants for the order in the home environment has been afforded to an officer of the responsible body.

## Who can be adopted?

Only a child under the age of 18 years who is not or has not been married can be adopted. An adopted child can be adopted again.

Where one, or both, of the applicants is the child's parent, step-parent or relative or the child was placed with the applicants by an adoption agency or under a High Court order an adoption order can only be made if the child is over 19 weeks old and at all times during the preceding 13 weeks has had his home with one or both of the applicants (Section 13(1)).

In all other cases the child must be at least 12 months old and must have lived with one or both of the applicants at all times during the previous 12 months (s 13(2)).

## Who can apply?

Married and single people can apply to adopt and can make single or joint applications.

A joint application can only be made by a married couple and both parties must be over 21 years except where one of them is the parent of the child then that person need only be 18 years old.

A single application can be made by a single person who must be at least 21 years. The person may be married or unmarried. If she is married then she must satisfy the court that her spouse cannot be found or they have separated and are living apart permanently or the spouse is incapable of making an application due to mental or physical ill-health.

If the single applicant is the parent of the child then she must satisfy the court that the other parent is dead or cannot be found or some other reason exists (and it must be recorded by the court) justifying the exclusion of the other parent (s 15(3)).

### Parental agreement

Before the court can make an adoption order it must have the agreement of a parent or guardian of the child. It is accepted that 'parent' includes any person who has parental responsibility for the child. This will be the married parents, a guardian, an unmarried mother, an unmarried father who has gained parental responsibility, a person with a residence order in effect with respect to the child, a local authority with a care order and anyone who holds an emergency protection order.

The mother of the child cannot give an effective consent until at least six weeks after the birth of her child (s 18(4)).

The court must be satisfied that the consent is freely given with full understanding of the situation and is unconditional and this is witnessed by the reporting officer who will also provide the court with a full report on the case.

The agreement must exist at the time the order is made but can be withdrawn at any time until then.

However, there will be times when the court will consider it necessary to dispense with parental agreement.

### Grounds for dispensing with parental agreement

The grounds are contained in s 16(2).

They are when a parent or guardian:

- cannot be found or is incapable of giving agreement;
- is withholding his agreement unreasonably;

- has persistently failed without reasonable cause to discharge his parental responsibility for the child;
- has abandoned or neglected the child;
- has persistently ill-treated the child;
- has seriously ill-treated the child.

## Parent cannot be found or is incapable of giving consent

In these circumstances enquiries must be made in an effort to trace the relevant persons to give them notice of the proposed adoption. If they cannot be found then their consent can be dispensed with. This is also permitted where their whereabouts are known but they cannot be contacted as in the case of *Re R (Adoption)* (1967). The parents could not be contacted due to the nature of the political regime in their country.

In *Re L (A Minor) (Adoption: Parental Agreement)* (1987) it was held that the natural mother was incapable of giving her consent as she was suffering from a mental disorder under the Mental Health Act 1983 and was unable to understand the consequences of the adoption.

## Parent is withholding his agreement unreasonably

When considering this ground the court must bear in mind that just the fact that the parent does not agree with the proposed adoption will not make it unreasonable. A number of considerations have to be kept in mind when deciding whether or not it is unreasonable.

The decision must be judged at the time of the hearing and an objective test used, ie would a reasonable parent withhold their consent? Also it must be remembered that the child's welfare is not to be considered as paramount as in this situation the parent is in danger of losing his parental responsibility and rights with respect to the child and must be able to intervene if he has reasonable grounds to do so and as such the child's welfare is not allowed to override all other factors.

Having said that the welfare is not paramount it must be seen as the most important factor and any reasonable parent would see it as such and would look to see if the child would benefit from adoption and if obvious advantages would arise then perhaps the parent should not withhold his consent.

However, just because a parent withholds his agreement it does not make it unreasonable. There can be any number of views taken by any number of people to a given situation and none of them need be unreasonable; they may be right or wrong but not necessarily unreasonable.

The court has to decide whether or not the decision on the case falls within this 'band' of reasonableness.

The leading case in this area is *Re W (An Infant)* (1972). This case concerned an unmarried mother who had put the child up for adoption within days of his birth. He had been placed with prospective adopters and the mother had agreed to the adoption but later withdrew her agreement. The child had been with the other family for 18 months by this time and they could offer him a stable home whereas the natural mother led an unstable lifestyle having to care for her other two children whilst living in one room, without a job and with little prospect of gaining one. There were serious doubts about her ability to cope and the child had settled well with the other family.

The House of Lords used the factors mentioned above to decide that the mother was unreasonably withholding her agreement.

It would be useful to compare the cases of *Re PA (An Infant)* (1971) and *Re D (An Infant) (Adoption: Parental Consent)* (1977).

In *Re PA* a young unmarried mother placed her baby for adoption due to pressure from relatives rather than through a real wish to do so. She later became engaged and felt able to care for the child and withdrew her agreement.

It was held that as the welfare of the child was not paramount it was reasonable for the mother to withhold her agreement. She had not truly wished to have her child adopted but had only done so because of family pressure. At the time the child was only one year old and any disruption caused by removing the child from the new family would be only temporary and the child would gain a benefit from its natural bond with the mother.

In *Re D* the child's parents divorced and the mother remarried and wished to adopt the child. The father, a practising homosexual, objected to the adoption.

It was held that a reasonable parent would consider the effect that his sexuality, and that of others with whom the boy would have contact, could have on the boy and would see that there would be advantages for the boy to be adopted by his mother who could provide a secure future.

It was unreasonable for the father to withhold his agreement.

152

## Parent has persistently failed without reasonable cause to discharge his parental responsibility for the child

This factor includes the statutory duty on the parent to maintain the child and also to show the normal love and affection expected from a parent to a child.

Both elements of this ground must be satisfied, ie the element of persistence and the element of 'without just cause'.

The element of 'persistence' must be seen in the sense of being permanent and complete to such a degree that there would be no advantage to the child in maintaining contact with the parent as was held in the case of *Re B (S) (An Infant) (No 2)* (1968) where a father had not sought access to the child for a number of years and had failed to enquire about her or to maintain her during that period.

The court held that he had washed his hands of her and dispensed with his consent.

*Re M (An Infant)* (1965) illustrates that where an unmarried mother had left her child with the proposed adopters to conceal the birth from her parents it was seen by the court that she had failed to carry out her parental duties 'with just cause'.

## Parent has abandoned or neglected the child

'Abandoned' in this sense would be equated with conduct that could render the parent liable to prosecution under the criminal law and is restrictively interpreted as is the term 'neglected'. Because of this approach this factor is rarely used in practice.

## Parent has persistently ill-treated the child

'Persistent' is treated as in the above factor, ie permanent and in the case of *Re A (A Minor) (Adoption: Dispensing with Agreement)* (1981) it was held that a child that had been severely and repeatedly assaulted over a three week period had been persistently ill-treated.

## Parent has seriously ill-treated the child.

Under this ground a single incident could lead the court to dispense with parental agreement if of a sufficiently serious nature, eg an incident of sexual abuse.

## Proposals for reform

Proposals for reform in the area of adoption have been published in the consultation paper 'Review of Adoption Law: Report to Ministers of an Inter-Departmental Working Group' and in the Government White Paper 'Adoption: the Future'.

An important element contained in these documents is that there should be an assimilation of the Children Act principles, ie those contained in s 1, the welfare principle, the delay principle and the 'no order' principle into adoption.

There would be a more common sense approach to the factors to be considered when dealing with adoption. This would include the ages of the parties wishing to adopt and their cultural or racial background. Although such matters would be still considered, the most important issue would be whether or not the prospective parents would be able to provide the necessary love and care for the child.

There is also a recommendation that there be a less restrictive approach to the matter of 'open' adoption, ie where contact is allowed between the child and the natural family. Research has shown that this would be beneficial to some children.

An important issue raised by these reports is that where the child involved is aged over 12 his wishes should be respected and he should be able to accept or reject the adoption. The court would only be able to dispense with his agreement if he was incapable of giving his agreement.

There would also be reform in the area of dispensing with parental agreement. The first ground, ie where they cannot be found/are incapable of giving their agreement would remain but then a new ground, that adoption would have greater advantages for the child than any other alternative, would be the only time that a court could dispense with parental agreement.

Whether or not these proposals come into effect is yet to be seen but it would seem sensible that the area of adoption should be brought into line with other areas of child law and, at least, be based on the basic principles of the Children Act.

# Revision Notes

## Public law

### Care and supervision orders

Who can apply? Section 31(1). Local authorities and NSPCC.
Threshold Criteria s 31(2). The only way to obtain a care order or a supervision order:

### Two part test
- The child is suffering/likely to suffer significant harm; and
- such harm is attributable to the level of care – objective test or the child is beyond control.

### Definition of term (s 31(9))
- 'Harm': ill-treatment or impairment of health and development.
- 'Development': physical, intellectual, emotional, social or behavioural development.
- 'Health': physical or mental health.
- 'Ill-treatment': includes sexual abuse and other forms of ill-treatment which are not physical.

  Time to consider 'significant harm' *Re M (A Minor) (Care Order: Threshold Conditions)* (1994).

### Effects of a care order
- Parental responsibility shared between the local authority and the parents.
- Local authority can limit the parents exercise of parental responsibility but only when shown to be necessary.
- Limits placed on local authority's powers re child's name, religion, adoption etc.
- Court should not seek to add conditions to a care order.
- Section 34 presumption of parental contact.

### Effects of a supervision order
- Local authority does not gain parental responsibility but the supervisor can give directions to the parties to try and achieve the best results from the order.
- Order lasts for one year but can be extended for up to three years.

### Interim care and supervision orders
- Such orders are avilable to the court and last for eight weeks but there is no limit on the number that can be granted.
- However bear s 1(2) – delay principle – in mind.

### Discharge of care and supervision orders
- Application by local authorities,persons with parental responsibility or the child (s 39).
- Other persons can apply for a residence order which if granted will discharge the care order (s 91(1)). They will require leave.

### Appointment of guardian *ad litem*
- Section 41(1) requires the appointment of a guardian *ad litem* if necessary to safeguard the child's interests.
- His general duty is to investigate the case and ascertaining the child's wishes and understanding.
- He will be independent ie not employed by the local authority involved in the proceedings.


## Emergency protection

### Child assessment orders (s 43(1))

### Who can apply? Local authorities and NSPCC
Three requirements – all need to be present:
- Reasonable cause to suspect signifcant harm.
- Assessment is required to determine whether or not harm is being suffered.
- Such an assessment would not be made without an order.

### Duration and directions
Seven days duration. Directions re who can assess, where it will be done and the type of assessment required ie medical or psychological assessment.

### Child's ability to refuse assessment if of sufficient understanding
If the court is satisfied it can treat the application as that for an emergency protection order if the grounds exist.

## Emergency protection orders

### Who can apply? Any person, local authority and NSPCC
Section 44(1)(a):

Reasonable cause to believe the child is likely to suffer significant harm if either:

(a) he is not removed to accommodation; or

(b) he does not remain where he is being accommodated.

Section 44(1)(b):

Local authority can apply if:

(a) making enquiries under s 47; and

(b) the enquiries are being frustrated by access being unreasonably refused and there is reasonable cause to believe that access is a matter of urgency.

*Ex parte* applications can be made.

### Duration
Eight days plus one extension of seven days which ensures that matters are dealt with without delay.

### Effects
- It allows removal/retention of the child.
- Directions can be given re contact and examinations.
- Child can refuse examination if of sufficient understanding.
- Local authority has limited parental responsibility for the duration of the order.
- No appeal is possible against an EPO but an application for discharge can be made after 72 hours.

# Wardship

- Family proceedings.
- Wardship and the Children Act 1989.
- Private law.
- No restrictions but consider s 8 orders and possible advantages.

  Public law restrictions placed on local authorities by s 100:
- They cannot use wardship to gain parental responsibility.
- Local authorities require leave to apply.
- Section 100(3) contains factors to be considered.

(a)  result required cannot be achieved by way of statutory code
(b)  there is reasonable cause to believe that the child would suffer significant harm if wardship is not exercised.

# Adoption

An adoption order ends natural parents' parental responsibility and vests it in the adoptive parents.

Section 6 states that the child's welfare is not paramount but is the first consideration.

### Freeing for adoption
Freeing orders made by local authorities

### Adoption orders:
* Who can be adopted? Children under 18.
* Who can adopt? Married and single applicants.

### Dispensing with parental agreement (s 16(2)).
Grounds
When a parent:
* cannot be found or is incapable of giving agreement;
* is withholding his agreement unreasonably;
* has persistently failed without reasonable cause to discharge his parental responsibility for the child;
* has abandoned or neglected the child;
* has persistently ill-treated the child;
* has seriously ill-treated the child.

### Proposals for reform
Assimilation of Children Act principles.
Basic decision to be based on what is best for the welfare of the child and the ability of the parents to care for the child.
Less restrictive approach to 'open' adoption.
New grounds for dispensing with parental agreement:
* cannot be found or is incapable of giving agreement;
* that adoption would have greater advantages for the child than any other alternative.

# Index